Rulebook
of a
Narcissist

Narcissism Self-help Guide

Happy and sad at the same time.

Sad, there is a need for education and support on the subject of narcissistic abuse.

Happy, I can play my part in this through both my books, blogs, emails, masterclasses and coaching sessions.

It is a way of making sense to what happened to me, it offers an opportunity to deeply connect with others and I can tap into my creativity, 'translating' information in accessible ways, showing how narcissism affects the well-being and happiness of lots of people.

Thank you to my mother, who shut my mouth, closed my heart and made me feel the most worthless person in the universe. But somehow, she also gave me the strength to fight the devastation and find a way forward that benefits me and lots of others.

Thank you, mum.

Published in 2021 Indie Publishing

ISBN 9798455389344

Cover design: Julia Britten JBS Design

Printed in Great Britain by
Biddles Books Limited, King's Lynn, Norfolk

Rulebook
of a
Narcissist

Narcissism Self-help Guide

Dr. Mariette Jansen

Author of bestseller
'From Victim to Victor – Narcissism Survival Guide'

Endorsements

Mariette's knowledge and passion for the topic oozes from every page. To write about such a complex subject, and make it flow so beautifully is admirable. From the first page to the last, I was absorbed and couldn't put the book down. So many people's lives will be enriched by this read. Well done, Mariette. Your first book was exceptional, your second is equally as noteworthy.

Angela W.

Sometimes you find a book and an author who "just makes sense". Rulebook is one of those books you can read in one sitting or easily flick through and read in bits. I've learnt something different each time I've picked it up. It's plain-speaking, which makes it easy to digest and understand. The examples given really helped me realise what I was dealing with and more importantly helped me recognise that it wasn't me that was the problem. I wholeheartedly recommend you take the time to read this book.

Wendy A.

A lovely laid-out book, which is easy on the eye.

The Rules are clearly expressed and straightforward to put into practice. This book is such a helpful tool to support you when faced with the duplicitous nature of a narcissist.

Stephanie H.

After having read Mariette's first book about narcissism. I was delighted she published another one. This is such an informative and easy to read book. I really feel I know them now.

As this book presents one rule at the time, it was as if it created space in my mind to think about it and process what it really meant for me. I took it one rule and one day at the time.

Beautifully presented and offering practical, very useful advice.

Leonie W.

I love, love, LOVE this book!

It is extremely well laid out, easy to follow & gets straight to the nub of things.

Dr Jansen's in-depth knowledge of narcissism and how to manage it shines through. Her authoritative voice on one of our 'least spoken about topics' – Narcissism - is very much needed in today's world.

This book is invaluable to me and helps me in my daily dealings with my narcissists.

Lorraine B.

This book will change your life! If only I had come across Mariette and this book 10 years ago…Finally someone who understands exactly what is going on and able to explain and coach me out of the toxicity which was a constant drain on me, my family and my every day life. Without Mariette's knowledge and expertise, I wouldn't be the person I am today.

Diana B.

Contents

Introduction

This book is to support anyone who has a narcissist in their life.

Or is interested in learning more about narcissism.

It will teach you how to recognise narcissistic behaviour and attitudes which prevent the development of a healthy relationship.

They are presented as rules, which are followed by guidance on how to respond in order to keep yourself safe and sane.

It is all about recognisable behaviour and grasping narcissism as an expression of behaviour and thought patterns.

Especially when dealing with narcissism, knowledge is power.

1

Who am I?

How much are you influenced by the people around you, the family you grew up in and the relationships and friendships you have formed along the way?

I believe life is aimed to be a range of lessons, encouraging us to grow and becoming more of our own person. In other words, becoming more authentic. To be authentic, you need to get rid of the 'noise on the line'. Noises are information and influences that aren't aligned with who you really are. They come from other people, social media, and society.

I had loads of noise on the line, that came from one person: my mother. She was or is (I don't know if she is still alive) the blueprint of a narcissist and was the centre of my universe. I spent most of my life trying to understand, and build a relationship with her.

It took me 58 years to get her noise out of my system and I still carry some residues. But those residues have been transformed into components that are truly me and the abuse I have suffered has resulted in me being authentically me. To get there, I had to cut the cords.

That was painful and difficult, but the best thing I have ever done.

As a life coach/psychotherapist, I worked with victims of emotional abuse, but while researching for my first self-help book on narcissism, I got to know the ins and outs of this condition and narcissistic abuse even better. I have connected with hundreds of people and discovered that most narcissists act in very similar ways. As if they were handed out a blueprint on how to behave and even what to say.

Based on those commonalities, I started to post my narcissist rules on social media.

I captured their behaviour, thinking patterns, values, and the way they treat their victims. It was light, but educational and easy to digest. Each rule was followed by a suggestion and helpful response, aimed at supporting victims in developing their skills on how to deal with narcissists.

This gentle style of education was well received, fun to create and ultimately led to this book.

It is my mission in life to offer information and education about Narcissistic Personality Disorder (NPD) and support victims on their journey to heal. As a life coach/psycho-therapist I have been able to design a special coaching programme to help people heal: Narcissistic Abuse Recovery Coaching.

In June 2020 I published my first book 'From Victim to Victor – Narcissism Survival Guide', which became a bestseller and I am very proud to say, got an award.

2

How to use this book

Narcissistic abuse is crippling, extremely damaging and difficult to understand.

This book aims to create more understanding of how narcissists operate, through an overview of their most common behaviours. No matter the circumstances or where they are in the world, their age, or gender, they speak the same language and act in a similar manner. I think of it as their rulebook and have put together 63 typical rules of narcissists.

Some of these rules are applicable to other type of abusers: bullies, coercive controllers, addicts and co-dependent abusers.

The rulebook offers an excellent starting point to recognise and start dealing with emotional abuse.

It is an accessible way to get a feel for the narcissist and their behaviours and get some suggestions on how to deal with those.

Narcissists operate on an instinctive level, aiming to survive. As in the animal world, only the fittest will survive, and the strongest will get the best food and gain the most power. That is how narcissists think and behave.

Knowing how narcissists think and behave will help you to take control in situations that are meant to control you. Being familiar with their rules will put you in a much stronger position.

Do you want to read this book from start to finish in one go?

That is one way.

But I suggest you apply each rule on your narcissist and make notes on how that rule comes to life. And for you to 'translate' the suggestion of the 'helpful response' in your own way.

3

Narcissism in a nutshell

People who suffer from narcissistic personality disorder (NPD) are called narcissists. As with any disorder, there is a sliding scale on a spectrum and most people will even recognise the odd narcissistic trait in themselves from time to time.

Showing a few traits doesn't make someone a narcissist or a danger to others. But specific traits are an indication of the level of NPD and the harm that could be done.

Narcissists or people with strong narcissistic tendencies are masters of manipulation and are keen to take charge of the important relationships in their lives. These could be their partners, children, or friends.

They control people and are good at creating relationships that serve their needs but are damaging for their counterparts. Narcissists are looking for people who deliver attention, admiration, and confirmation. They need this to feel good and it is called Narcissistic Supply. It is an addiction and as with any addiction, after the one fix another one is required. They are never satisfied.

The manipulative and controlling behaviour of a narcissist is motivated by:

Getting their Narcissistic Supply.

Hiding their fragile ego, in order to feel safe.

The five main characteristics of a narcissist

1. **A narcissist has a grandiose view of themselves and are the centre of the universe**

    Even though they are convinced they are fabulous and interesting, they are needy for attention as a means of confirmation and admiration. This is why they are not only the centre of their own universe; they need to be the centre of other people's universe as well.

2. **A narcissist has a sense of entitlement**

    Because of their grandiosity and importance, they expect to be overindulged, waited on hand and foot, without the need to appreciate what others do for them. It is the way it should be in their view of the world.

3. **A narcissist will control and manipulate people, situations and the truth**

    As the Narcissistic Supply is their life force, it is crucial to them that they get it. To guarantee this, they aim to take control on all possible levels.

4. **A narcissist can't handle criticism**

    In their delusional vision of themselves, it is impossible that something about them wouldn't be right . The mere idea of this would spark the fear that their fragile ego is being exposed, which for them needs to be avoided at all costs.

5. **A narcissist lacks empathy and emotional awareness**

    It is easy for them to be very cruel and malicious because they don't feel guilt or remorse. They also can't understand other people's feelings. The only person they feel for is themselves.

If someone shows all five of the above characteristics, they are most likely suffering from narcissistic personality disorder. They will cause harm and pain to others, which makes it dangerous to be around them.

When dealing with a narcissist and trying to understand the motivation for their actions, it makes sense to bring it back to their need for the Narcissistic Supply and the fear of being discovered.

Who is your narcissist?

In this day and age I am willing to bet that everyone has at least one narcissist in their lives. Maybe you are not that affected by them. Maybe you shrug what happens off as not important. But it is still important to recognise them. Because when you are vulnerable, they will get at you.

The following quiz will help you to find out whether the unpleasant person you are thinking of might be a narcissist.

The quiz will help you recognise some traits and is not a diagnostic tool.

Have someone in mind (MN – My Narcissist) when answering the following questions:

1.	I often feel uncomfortable in the presence of MN	Yes / No
2.	MN is very critical of me	Yes / No
3.	I never know what mood MN is in	Yes / No
4.	MN is not kind and caring towards me	Yes / No
5.	MN applies double standards: what I have to adhere to is not applicable to MN	Yes / No
6.	The conversation always revolves around MN	Yes / No
7.	I am nervous because it feels as if I am always doing the wrong thing (according to MN)	Yes / No
8.	I find it hard to trust MN	Yes / No
9.	I often give in to keep the peace	Yes / No
10.	MN always wants me to agree with them	Yes / No

If MN scores a few yesses, it might be relevant to learn more about MN. Maybe that they are just annoying, or maybe that they apply a lot more narcissist rules than you had anticipated.

Either way, don't entirely make up your mind straight away.

Read, learn, recognise, observe and then conclude.

Excellence is a value, perfectionism is an insecurity.

Dr Mariette Jansen

4

The main values of a narcissist

Values are basic and fundamental beliefs that guide and motivate attitudes or actions. They help you to determine what is important to you. Values are personal qualities you aspire to have, becoming the person you want to be. They inform how you treat yourself and others, how you interact with others and the world around you and help you make decisions. Values are the foundation of all you are doing and thinking. They are usually positive and capture beliefs about what is right and wrong, providing a moral compass and your deeper drivers.

Examples of values are love, respect, trust, loyalty, honesty, integrity, caution, financial security, justice, equality, reliability and family.

Values exist whether you are aware of them or not. When what you do and how you behave matches your values, life feels good. There is a sense of contentment, safety, and satisfaction. You don't have external 'noise' on the line.

But when your actions aren't aligned with your values, you don't feel happy. There is a sense of discomfort because something doesn't feel quite right.

For you.

Examples

When reliability is one of your values it is important for you to stick to your appointments. You wouldn't change your plans because something else came up that might be more fun. It is imperative you are on time, which also stems from your value of being reliable.

Imagine the challenge where you have to choose between honesty and loyalty. A good friend confides having an affair with another friend's husband. Which value prevails? Are you loyal to the one who confided or is it more important to be honest?

When your values are violated, you will feel uncomfortable at best and unhappy and guilty at worst.

How values affect your relationships

It is easy to relate to people who embrace similar values. It offers safety, connection, recognition, and validation. The blueprint is in place, and you can start building a relationship straight away.

If you fall in love with someone who isn't on the same par with your values, trouble is on the horizon. Imagine you embrace the value of family and are keen to build your own and your potential partner is not having any of it. What are the changes for a steady, long-lasting, and fulfilling relationship?

Imagine the entrepreneur who sets up his business, based on his main values 'nature' and 'mental health'. His business mission is: 'Adding value to someone's life and mental condition through offering an accessible experience of nature'. The business is all about physical activities in a natural environment: paddle boarding 'cruises', canoeing in the wild, tracking adventures and the like. He then attracted a potential business partner and soon discovered it would never work between them. Why? Because this person's main aim and value was 'making money'. There is nothing wrong with striving to make money, but it didn't match the value of the founder, so they agreed to part company.

Which are the most important values, embraced by a narcissist?

Any narcissist has two strong motivators that inform all their actions, and values are connected with these.

The first is the need for attention, admiration, and confirmation that they are the best (Narcissistic Supply). The second is the urge to hide their fragile ego, to keep themselves safe from being exposed as insecure or less good than they portray.

The moral direction of a narcissist is very different from that of 'normal' people, and when dealing with them it is helpful to keep in mind that you don't share the same values. Narcissists are playing games all the time and they manipulate any aspect in life. So, it might take you some time to become aware of their values.

If you have done the quiz, you will know your MN (My Narcissist).

Why not focus on discovering their values?

The following values are typical for someone who suffers from narcissistic personality disorder:

1. **Image and appearance**

   It is of the greatest importance to come across as beautiful, rich, intelligent, well-connected, and successful. A narcissist will sacrifice values such as financial security, family and reliability over image and appearance. This is what gives them confidence, and at the same time it is the way they mask their lack of it. A narcissist will easily change commitments if that results in more Narcissistic Supply. They step away from people who love them when they feel that their image is threatened. This happens when a family member gets more successful than they are. It is also common to getting into debt to show off the latest car or designer gadget. Narcissists will go on holiday to a resort that oozes posh and glamour. Even if they can only afford being there in a tent, 20 miles further out. They will still mention that they went to St Tropez.

2. Disrespect

There is only respect for their own needs, and in order to have those met they will disrespect anything else, such as other people's perspectives (they are not willing or able to see another perspective), boundaries (their sense of entitlement will push down the boundaries), people (no one is important apart from them). It can be quite shocking to hear how they put down their partners or the way they discredit other people through negativity and lies. Another way of disrespect is around boundaries and they happily reveal personal information in order to feel better about themselves.

3. Dishonesty

The truth is only the truth if it serves a purpose in the world of the narcissist. There is no factual truth, just their vision of what will enhance and ensure that their needs are met. They lie, twist and reframe without seeing that as dishonesty. It is from their perspective a necessity to keep themselves safe. It is not for nothing that they are called delusional, as even when there is evidence, they will stick to their story and truth.

4. Self-centredness

For the narcissist, the world revolves around them, and everyone who happens to be part of that world should go along with it. All events, situations and stories have them as the centrepiece. Their actions are focused on manufacturing this. One client told me how the eulogy his narcissistic father wrote for his mother was, apart from the first few sentences, all about him. Narcissists love creating drama with themselves in the main role. One client told me how her mother always got hysterically upset during family parties, so people were running up to her, soothing her and afterwards calling her to check on her. Such lovely attention at the expense of the party hosts.

5. Disloyalty

People can't be trusted. People are there to be used and if they don't fulfil their purpose anymore it is time to find someone else who can replace them. There is no recognition of the worth of shared experiences. It is very common that a narcissistic ex-partner will be involved within weeks with someone new. Narcissists are also known to be unfaithful and sometimes their reasons have to do with being jealous about another relationship. Their flirtation and seduction is not only to get their Narcissistic Supply, but also to destroy for others what seems to be good.

6. Control

It is extremely important for the narcissist to be in control. In control of themselves, as they need to protect their fragile ego, and in control of the people around them who need to give them their Narcissistic Supply. The supply doesn't need to be given naturally; it can easily be forced. The narcissist doesn't care how they get it. A favourite method to control is to confuse. People who are confused give in readily. How confusing is it when people (narcissists) change their behaviour and ideas all the time? Today they love you, tomorrow they hate you. Today they love going out, tomorrow they hate it. Today their favourite colour is blue, tomorrow it is green. They make people doubt themselves, which makes it easier to control them.

7. Self-importance

It is only the narcissist who counts. The whole of their life and that of others is organised, controlled and bullied around the importance of the narcissist. The lack of empathy, let alone compassion, makes it impossible for them to connect to the emotions and upset of others and makes it easier to focus on the self. Narcissists don't love people; they love what people can do for them.

When dealing with a narcissist, it is important to know where they are coming from. They think, feel, and behave very differently from other people and this unfortunately can be very damaging to others. Imagine that you, with your values of honesty, respect, and love, communicate with a narcissist, who will respond from their opposite values of dishonesty, disrespect and self-importance. The exchange will be incongruent and never lead to a satisfying communication, let alone a satisfying relationship.

People get involved with narcissists because they put on a mask and seem charming, generous and fun. In a romantic relationship this is at the start and it's called love bombing. They apply this behaviour just long enough to hook someone in and then they change. With that starts the confusion. How can someone who was so loving and attentive become vile, moody, and unpleasant? The answer can be traced back to their values.

Whenever you feel uncomfortable with another person (colleague, boss, family member, partner, friend), discover their values and compare those with yours. This will give you a good handle to notice the differences between you.

5

The thinking patterns of a narcissist

Introduction

The number of times my clients tell me a story and then make comments along the lines of: 'I can't believe he said that?' or 'How can a mother think like that?' or 'I don't get that she doesn't see the seriousness of the situation?'

Narcissists will never cease to surprise people who don't think like them. People such as their victims.

Narcissist's mental make-up is different from 'normal' people. Their thinking pattern is very simple and straightforward. The issue is that it is difficult for non-narcissists to put on a narcissistic thinking cap, as it is so far outside of their way of thinking.

Simple and clear

To get a grip on your dealings with a narcissist it is important to understand the driving thoughts of people with narcissistic personality disorder or those with strong narcissistic traits. Their thoughts are pretty straightforward, they are just different.

1. **I am the best and the only one who is important**

    This can translate into being the best in politics, the prettiest on the team, the most intelligent in the department, the most important family member, the richest guy around and so on.

The starting point of any line of thought is that they are the best and the most important. It is also the end point of any line of thought.

This taps into their values of image, self-centredness, and self-importance.

2. **There is only black and white**

Grey areas are a no-go territory. Grey is confusing and can undermine the statement that 'I am the best'. A narcissist is very simple and clear in their opinion. Once they have an opinion, they stick to it. Reconsidering and discussing the pros and cons is not an option. The world is how they have defined it.

They divide the world into winners, which they clearly are, and losers. Even when they lose, they will give it a twist, so they can still consider themselves as the winner. In their mind, them losing will be down to other people misbehaving or cheating.

The connecting values are dishonesty and control.

3. **You are with me or against me**

Narcissists judge people on their ability to give them what they need: attention, admiration, and confirmation. Their victims are all expected to offer the Narcissistic Supply and should be in the camp that is 'with me'. Some of these are chosen to become a 'flying monkey'. Flying monkeys are the allies of narcissists. They are expected to be supportive and act on their behalf, usually for abusive purposes. They have been lured in via 'poor me' stories, where the narcissist portrays to have been treated badly by someone else. The flying monkeys try to save the narcissist by becoming their advocate.

People who are 'against' them and hold different opinions are qualified as losers and enemies. Narcissists happily create smear campaigns, undermine whatever their enemies stand for and will cut their head off (allegorically) in order to feel taller. The enemy deserves punishment and narcissists are experts at finding punishments that really hurt.

The values that underpin this thought are disrespect, self-importance, and disloyalty.

4. The only truth is my truth

Narcissists are delusional in their perception and interpretation of events. They won't let the objective truth get in the way of their view of the world. And their view always serves their idea of 'I am the best'. With that comes 'I am always right'. They can't deal with criticism and negative feedback. It makes them angry and aggressive. And they have the ability to reframe situations, twist what happened or bluntly lie in order to be right.

It is not possible to have a respectful discussion where you challenge their opinions. That is felt as an attack, which makes you the enemy, and you will be on the receiving end of their punishment.

The values of control, dishonesty and self-importance underpin this thought.

5. I don't care about you, I only care about me

Narcissists lack empathy and emotional awareness. There are several studies that suggest they miss the part of the brain that regulates empathy. It makes them dangerous. Their lack of emotional awareness blocks them from realising how poorly they behave towards other people. There are plenty of examples where people have been physically hurt or neglected by a narcissist without them thinking that they did anything wrong.

Values connected with this thought are image and appearance, self-centredness, and self-importance.

Imagine an encounter with a narcissistic boss

You have prepared a proposal to change the distribution of a product. What you didn't know was that the original logistics were designed by your boss a few years ago. Your boss thinks 'I am the best'. Therefore, his logistics were the best and your proposal is attacking his position. He is not able to consider a slight change because his thinking is black and white. Your proposal means you have become the enemy and you are in for a punishment: put downs, smear campaigns and impossible assignments. He will reframe your proposal to kill it off.

Imagine being in a relationship with a narcissist

Your partner loves talking about herself and her assets or achievements. She is the best. At the start of the relationship, you thought that was very endearing, but now it has become irritating as she always seems to need to be the best. At everything. No grey, no 'room for improvement', only perfection. Disagreeing isn't an option because she'll make your life hell through her punishments: silent treatment, insults, no sex. Talking about it doesn't work. Her view of the world means that she is always right and she doesn't care that she is emotionally hurting you, that your confidence is drained and that you are upset.

Imagine a country being led by a narcissist

This person would be on a personal journey looking for personal glory. Acting out the 'I am the best' mantra and shouting out clear statements that leave no room for shades of grey: 'The refugees are at fault, the socialists are wrong, all women are monkeys'. They will attract a following of people who are looking to simplify their lives (this was one of the attractions of Hitler, according to Dr Craig Malkin).

In order to be 'the best' the truth will be manipulated to suit the story of the leader, and anyone who gets in the way will be punished (Hitler shot people or sent them off to concentration camps).

'Narcissists will never let the truth get in the way of the story that suits them'

Dr Mariette Jansen

6

The rulebook

Introduction

Narcissists show incredible similarities in thoughts and behaviour.

Those similarities are the basis for this rulebook. I have collected these rules over time, talking to people, listening to my clients and checking other sources. All the 'rules' have popped up several times with different people in different circumstances and are therefore marked as typical of narcissistic thinking and behaviour.

Narcissists aim to impress the outside world and confuse their inner sanctum. They will never stop to surprise, but if you can grab their ideas upfront, the surprises will shock you less and maybe evoke an 'aha' (I have read or heard this before) reaction.

Knowing their rules helps you to prepare your responses and be less vulnerable.

Rules are red flags and mostly the result of what narcissists are focused on:

Getting their Narcissistic Supply. They need your attention – even if it is negative attention – admiration, and confirmation. They manipulate others into behaviour that satisfies their supply.

Protecting their fragile ego. They are wearing their mask, pretending to be on top of their game, but they work at this all the time. They need to communicate that they are better than anyone else. Often that means telling others how useless they are. Their life is one long search for external validation and perfection.

How many rules?

I started with over one hundred and noticed some overlap and similarities between them. Based on the meaning of 63 I decided to stick to this number: according to numerology the number 63 represents humanitarianism, harmony, balance, tolerance, idealism and family. Being a blend of the numbers 9, 6 and 3, this number signifies compassion, optimism, and healing. Exactly what people who are affected by narcissists need the most from themselves and for themselves.

Type of rules

To create some order, I have divided the rules in 4 types: the ones relating to a description of a narcissist, the description of their victim through the eyes of the narcissist, how they treat their victim and how they think the relationship should work.

Each rule is written from the perspective of the narcissist and the helpful response is written from the perspective of the person who is on the receiving end of their narcissist's behaviour.

Each response aims to give a perspective or suggestion.

What would keep you safe?

What would limit the damage?

How can you step from an emotional 'shock' into your rational thinking?

As life in the presence of a narcissist is full of surprises, there is no way these responses can cater for every situation. But they give a guideline, an idea or inspiration to step away from the control of your narcissist.

Rulebook
of a
Narcissist

Trust is earned,
respect is given,
loyalty is demonstrated.
Betrayal of any of these means
losing all three.

Rule series 1

The big, most important, and interesting rules:
All about ME, myself and I

These are rules that narcissists use to describe themselves.

How they think about themselves, their behaviour, principles, opinions, and perceptions.

It is helpful to know where narcissists are coming from and how they operate in the world.

These rules are connected with the values of image and appearance, self-centredness, and self-importance.

1.   I am better than everybody else and certainly miles better than you

2.   I am perfect, always right and don't need to change

3.   I thrive on the misery of others

4.   I don't acknowledge or respect boundaries

5.   Give me your finger and I will bite off your hand

6.   Everybody values me

7. Feelings make me uncomfortable

8. I make everyone wait for me

9. I deny any fact, situation or event that doesn't serve me

10. I never apologise

11. I am above rules, policies and the law

12. I don't care about anyone but me

13. I have the emotional maturity of a toddler

14. My mask is my most important accessory

15. I steal and hide stuff to confuse and upset

16. I am extremely critical of others

17. I create drama to ensure that I am centre stage

18. I refuse to line up in a queue

19. I will never forget anything I can use against someone else

20. I tell others how to act and behave

21. I choose a profession that gives me status

22. I take credits for the achievements of others

23. I am always campaigning to get people in my tribe

> **RULEBOOK OF A NARCISSIST**
> **01**
>
> *I am better than everybody else and certainly miles better than you*

Narcissists are convinced they are special and superior to others. When they face a situation where they might not be seen as better, richer, or more interesting they usually withdraw and comment negatively on that particular situation.

If you are a partner, friend, or family member of a narcissist, they will blatantly tell you that they will always outshine you. If someone excels in their career, education, or sports, they will find a way to take the spotlight. They can't accept being outperformed. The worst case scenario is when it is crystal clear that they are not the best, they will then ignore the situation or twist the truth. Think of Donald Trump denying he lost the election in 2020 in the United States, while evidence showed it was clearly the case.

This rule is routed in the values of self-importance and image and appearance.

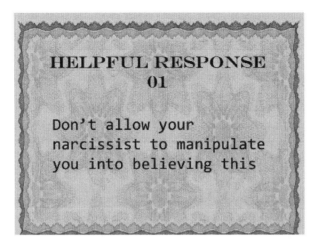

**HELPFUL RESPONSE
01**

Don't allow your
narcissist to manipulate
you into believing this

Not just that they are always better, but especially the way they devalue you. Life is not about being better than someone else. This is the thought pattern of an insecure person, like your narcissist, who put others down in order to elevate themselves.

Their remark is due to their issues; don't make those issues yours.

Remind yourself of your qualities and achievements and embrace them.

RULEBOOK OF A NARCISSIST
02

I am perfect, always right and don't need to change

Perfectionism is a sign of insecurity. Appearance and impressions are important for narcissists. They see themselves as perfect, which is their shield to hide their fragile ego. They are always right, which means no one is allowed to challenge them and it gives them that sense of authority, which they thrive on. Narcissists will never contemplate changing. They are stuck in their personal conviction of their perfectionism.

A huge challenge for narcissists is being disputed. It taps into their fear of being exposed and their low self-esteem needs to be hidden at all times. It is hidden so deeply that they themselves can't even access it.

This rule relates to the thought that they are the best.

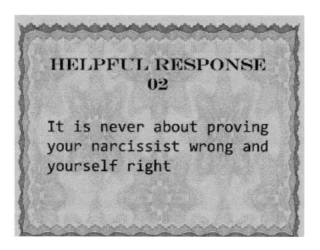

HELPFUL RESPONSE
02

It is never about proving
your narcissist wrong and
yourself right

If you challenge your narcissist, you are in for a battle which you will always lose

Your narcissist is closed off. Their eyes, ears and mind are not willing to receive any message that challenges them.

For them, change is sign of weakness. It is admitting that something could be done better. At times, they are able to change their behaviour, but that is only superficial and temporary. Underneath they will still embrace themselves as perfect and right.

Never anticipate profound change in your narcissist. They are set in their perfect ways and will stay put.

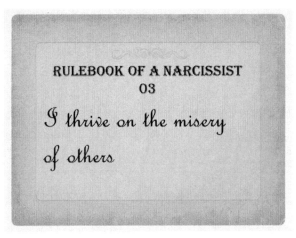

RULEBOOK OF A NARCISSIST
03

I thrive on the misery of others

Narcissists can't get enough of stories about horrible things that have happened to others.

The German word is Schadenfreude, which means pleasure that comes from witnessing the troubles, failures or humiliation of other people.

Tales about illness, family dramas or business misfortunes are shared with great delight. It is after all a confirmation that they are in a much better place than those unlucky ones.

I know a few narcissists who love reading about experiences of prisoners of war in the German concentration camps. And then talk about all the horrendous details.

It is down to their lack of empathy and the thought that others don't count. It explains how some narcissists can be extremely cruel to others, just for their own entertainment.

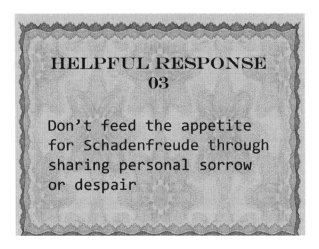

**HELPFUL RESPONSE
03**

Don't feed the appetite
for Schadenfreude through
sharing personal sorrow
or despair

Be careful with what you share as your narcissist will not support you, but actually enjoy your distress.

Don't expect support or kindness.

They can't give it.

Their enjoyment in your pain and the lack of empathy prevents this.

Find other people to confide in if you want to keep yourself safe from your narcissist's harming responses.

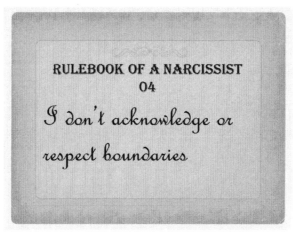

RULEBOOK OF A NARCISSIST
04

I don't acknowledge or respect boundaries

Narcissists ignore boundaries as these get in the way of what they are aiming for.

If someone sets a boundary, it limits their options to manipulate and control.

And it might feel to them that they are controlled.

They will do anything to challenge those boundaries: arguing, blaming, ridiculing, acting like a victim or raging.

And of course, not respecting them.

The connecting values are disrespect and control.

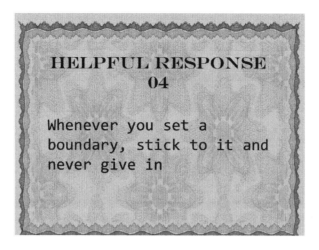

**HELPFUL RESPONSE
04**

Whenever you set a
boundary, stick to it and
never give in

Setting a boundary for your narcissist is challenging for both of you.

It might spark anger in your narcissist when you present your boundaries.

Therefore, communicate them clearly, firmly, and concisely and mention the consequences when they overstep them.

An example is that you set a boundary about a topic of conversation, which always leads to an argument. You might say that you don't want to talk about it anymore and if your narcissist still brings it up, you will hang up the phone, walk out of the room, or totally ignore them.

They will try to have their own way.

You are not allowed to set the terms, only they can do so.

However, if you stick to your guns, they ultimately have no choice but to give in.

RULEBOOK OF A NARCISSIST

05

Give me your finger and
I will bite off your hand

Narcissists are greedy and never satisfied.

Whatever is on offer, they always need more.

They operate like addicts.

They might be satisfied for a little while, but then the requirement for more crops up.

Topping up the supply of attention, admiration, and confirmation.

The control will get stronger, the abuse will get nastier, the suffocation worse.

Until their victim is broken.

Your narcissist doesn't value you or your efforts.

They don't consider your kindness.

They only see their own immediate satisfaction.

Which wears off pretty quickly, and then they come back for more.

The moment you open the door to give more, they will push the door off its hinges and grab everything they can.

It is easy for your narcissist as there is no empathy and no recognition of boundaries (Rule 4 'I don't acknowledge or respect boundaries')

But it is very hard for you.

Make a conscious decision on what and how much to give to your narcissist, have boundaries in place and don't allow them to step over those.

'What have I done to deserve this?

As my daughter I expect you to at least offer:

Some help,

Some attention,

Some money.'

Which translates as:

'I have never done anything to deserve anything.

But as I am very special, I am entitled to

A lot of your help,

All of your attention,

All of your money,

An anything else I can suck out of you.'

Dr Mariette Jansen

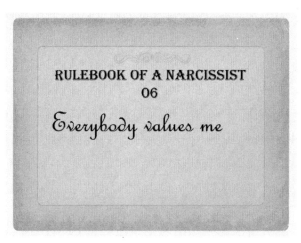

RULEBOOK OF A NARCISSIST
06

Everybody values me

Narcissists need to remind the people around them of their 'wonderfulness' and truly believe that others hold them in high regard. Of course, they like to hear it, but they also don't shy away from mentioning it themselves.

It is one of their ways of getting validation and feeling good.

It is the voice that silences the underlying insecurity.

'Everyone thinks I am intelligent.'

'I am brilliant in business.'

'Do you know how much money I have?'

The value of image and appearance is underlying these remarks.

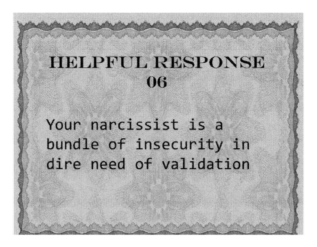

HELPFUL RESPONSE
06

Your narcissist is a
bundle of insecurity in
dire need of validation

When your narcissist is your romantic partner, you might have admired their intelligence, business acumen and wealth at the start of the relationship. But over time you have discovered more traits that you might find less admirable.

However, when your narcissist asks for validation, it works best to just give in and see them as a little child that needs a pat on the head.

Rule 13 'I have the emotional maturity of a toddler'

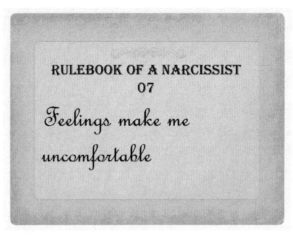

RULEBOOK OF A NARCISSIST

07

Feelings make me uncomfortable

Narcissists only recognise feelings of anger, fear, hate, and jealousy, or any variation of those.

They don't feel empathy, love, or kindness and have no emotional awareness (the ability to recognise and make sense of not just your own emotions, but also those of others).

According to research in Germany (Medical University Berlin), narcissists lack the relevant area in the brain that is connected with empathy and loving emotions.

When a person shows feelings that are unfamiliar to narcissists, it makes them feel insecure as they have no idea what is going on.

They deal with it by ignoring and dismissing positive and real emotions.

> ## HELPFUL RESPONSE
> ## 07
>
> Emotions are unchartered territory for your narcissist and this prevents a deep emotional connection

Your narcissist lacks emotional awareness. They don't recognise feelings in themselves and consequently can't acknowledge them in you. If you try to share your feelings, you will hit a brick wall and will never get through.

The only way for them to 'deal' with your emotions is through denial, ignoring or ridiculing.

Dismissing you as overexcited or oversensitive.

Your narcissist will react with 'You are hysterical' or tell you to stop crying.

Don't expect kindness or consolation.

It is important to know that emotional intimacy is not possible with your narcissist.

To keep yourself safe, refrain from sharing your deep feelings as you will only get hurt.

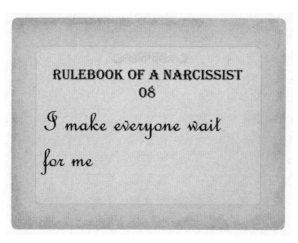

RULEBOOK OF A NARCISSIST
08

I make everyone wait

for me

Making people wait for you means that you have their attention.

They will be thinking about you, and they may be annoyed but all their energy is focused on the one who hasn't arrived yet.

That is the position narcissists love.

Being in the forefront of people's minds.

Often, they are the last to show up and bathe in the attention that comes with this.

When asked to do something, they will usually answer along the lines of 'wait a minute' which translates as 'don't think that what I will do for you is more important than what I am doing right now for myself'. Or when picking someone up, they are always a few minutes too late.

Again, it's forcing the fix of the attention, coming from their value of self-importance and the thought that 'I am the only one who is important'.

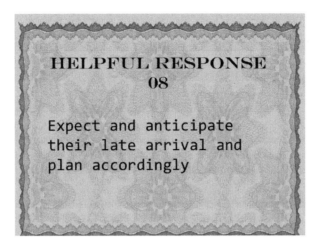

HELPFUL RESPONSE
08

Expect and anticipate
their late arrival and
plan accordingly

There is nothing else to do other than to anticipate your narcissist's lateness.

Avoid being irritated or annoyed, as this will only spark an argument.

If you stay with your narcissist, it is something you have to get used to as it will never change.

RULEBOOK OF A NARCISSIST
09

I deny any fact, situation or event doesn't serve me

Narcissists lie easily: 'We never had that conversation, I didn't receive a letter and that event never took place'.

They are so used to lying that their perception of reality is delusional as they believe their own lies, which makes it impossible to have normal conversations.

Even when there is proof of their lies, like text messages or emails, they will continue to deny it.

Their truth is the only truth in their thinking pattern and the values dishonesty and image support this thought.

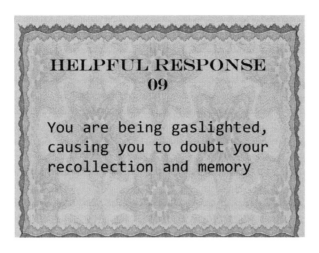

HELPFUL RESPONSE
09

You are being gaslighted,
causing you to doubt your
recollection and memory

Even though you and others might know that your narcissist is lying, there is no way to convince them.

This is what they do to protect themselves.

This is how they look after themselves.

They won't let reality get in the way of their secure position.

If possible, record events and situations with minute detail and when you doubt yourself, you can consult your notes to affirm the reality.

Preventing you from thinking you are going mad.

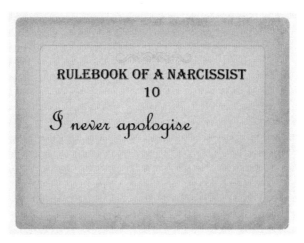

RULEBOOK OF A NARCISSIST
10

I never apologise

An apology is an acknowledgement of having done something wrong.

As narcissists are perfect, they never do anything wrong.

Therefore, there is never a need to apologise.

If they can't escape giving an apology, it will never be genuine and sound like: 'I am sorry if you thought I did something wrong' or 'I am sorry that you are so sensitive'.

In the way they phrase it, they make sure the other party is seen as the one in the wrong.

It is never them.

**HELPFUL RESPONSE
10**

Never expect a sincere
apology

The lack of empathy and boundaries will make it impossible for your narcissist to recognise when they are being unreasonable or even at fault.

They simply don't get it.

Even when it has been explained several times in different ways, the penny won't drop.

Simply because your narcissist is not open to the option that they might have done something wrong.

An apology from your narcissist will only happen when they can't avoid it and it will never be genuine.

RULEBOOK OF A NARCISSIST

11

I am above rules, policies and the law

Narcissists set rules for other people.

Rules that need to be obeyed.

But rules set by others, even the law, don't apply to them.

They are above the law, too special to adhere to what others have set out.

It is another way of showing the world that they are superior and above everyone else.

During the Covid pandemic many narcissists have ignored lockdown instructions.

Consider Rule 18 'I refuse to line up in a queue'.

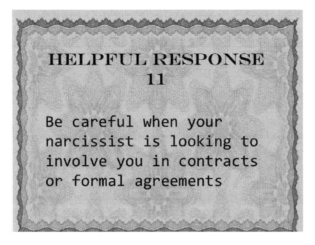

HELPFUL RESPONSE
11

Be careful when your
narcissist is looking to
involve you in contracts
or formal agreements

As your narcissist is above the law, you could endanger yourself if you don't do your own research.

Don't trust them.

Don't take their word for it.

When getting involved in formal or legal arrangements, make sure you consult your own, independent experts.

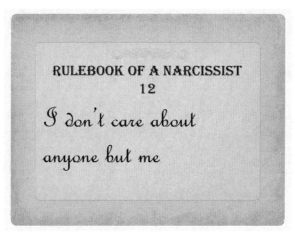

RULEBOOK OF A NARCISSIST
12

I don't care about anyone but me

Narcissists only care about themselves and see themselves as the centre of the universe.

They don't have a sense of the real world, as everything revolves around them.

As a consequence, no one is important but themselves.

All their choices confirm that their life is only about them.

Thanks to their lack of empathy, it is easy to act out this rule, as they can't imagine how it feels when they cause hurt or upset.

Narcissists are known to be extremely successful in business as they bypass the challenges that come with thinking of others.

Life is about them.

Never about others.

The motivation for everything your narcissist says and does is to benefit themselves.

In order to see clearly, remind yourself of this and you will better understand what is behind their actions.

Even if it is wrapped up as kindness or thoughtfulness, at the end of the day it is about them and only them.

It is never about anyone else.

It is never about you.

You only count as a supplier and when you stop, you will be replaced.

It is tough, but it is the truth.

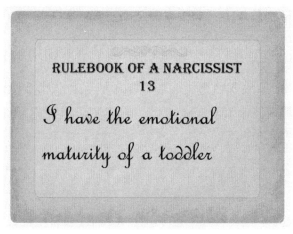

RULEBOOK OF A NARCISSIST
13

I have the emotional
maturity of a toddler

Narcissist's range of emotions is limited to anger, fear, hate, and jealousy and variations of those.

When any of these feelings are sparked, their reactions are instant and impulsive.

Like a toddler.

They throw a tantrum, blaming and screaming.

Sometimes their tantrum turns into an aggressive outburst, which seems totally over the top. This is called narcissistic rage.

Aiming to get their way and force their will upon others.

Like a toddler, narcissists are not able to think rationally when they are upset.

**HELPFUL RESPONSE
13**

When your narcissist is
raging, keep yourself
safe and don't engage

When your narcissist is in this emotional space, it is not possible to reach them.

Allow them to vent their energy, but make sure you are safe.

When you try to discuss this afterwards, your narcissist might make excuses along the lines of 'it wasn't too bad' and 'it was really you who caused my anger'.

Don't expect your narcissist to take responsibility for their behaviour.

Narcissistic rage and your fear are an indication of how unhealthy the relationship with your narcissist is.

RULEBOOK OF A NARCISSIST
14

My mask is my most important accessory

Narcissists behave differently behind closed doors, where they show their real personality, than in the outside world.

This is where they wear a mask, or false persona, acting as a kind and attentive person who is generous and fun.

The mask hides their vulnerability, protects them from criticism and challenges, and supports them in getting lots of positive attention and confirmation.

This mask also prevents their victims from getting support for their situation when they talk to others.

Others see the narcissist as a great person and won't believe what the victim tells them.

> ### HELPFUL RESPONSE
> ### 14
>
> Be mindful that people
> may not see your
> narcissist the way you
> know them. Check before
> you confide

Living with a narcissist is a lonely existence, as most people don't understand the extent and the viciousness of the abuse.

If you want to talk to friends or family, make sure they are open to your experiences and grasp what is going on.

Otherwise, you will feel even more confused and alone.

This is one of the aims of your narcissist: to alienate you from your friends and family in order to make it easier to control you.

Talking to people who understand is also possible via a range of forums on Facebook. This can be a real lifesaver.

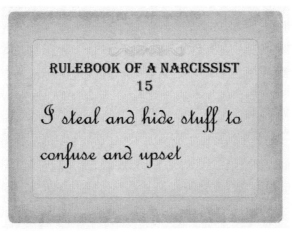

RULEBOOK OF A NARCISSIST
15
I steal and hide stuff to confuse and upset

Narcissists love creating upheaval and feeling in control.

One way of gaslighting and confusing is taking things away, putting them in different places and pretending it is their victim who must have done it.

They want to make their victims feel like 'I am going mad'.

Passports disappear to prevent a trip abroad, keys are put in a different place, food goes missing.

Narcissists love playing these games.

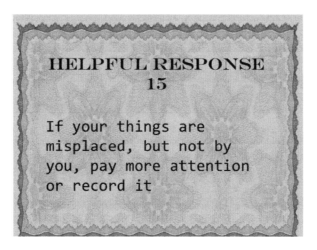

**HELPFUL RESPONSE
15**

If your things are
misplaced, but not by
you, pay more attention
or record it

Your narcissist enjoys unsettling you by making changes in your direct environment.

Gaslighting stems from a 1944 movie entitled *Gaslight*, in which a manipulative husband tries to make his wife think she is losing her mind by making subtle changes in her environment, including slowly and steadily dimming the flame of a gas lamp.

Your narcissist wants to confuse you but might also steal or hide your stuff to spoil something you like, such as the ticket for a concert. This behaviour is inspired by Rule 52 'If I can't have it, you can't have it either.'

Protect yourself from this abuse by keeping everything that is important to you in a place your narcissist doesn't have access to.

If you are considering leaving your narcissist, make sure that important paperwork and personal items are in a safe place, out of reach of your narcissist.

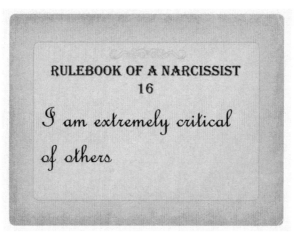

RULEBOOK OF A NARCISSIST
16

I am extremely critical of others

Of course, narcissists are critical of others, quick to insult and respond aggressively to perceived criticism. This is all to do with their value of self-importance and the thought pattern around their grandiosity.

They use this as a tool to sow seeds of doubts in the mind of their victims around family, friends, and colleagues. It is part of the alienation process to single out their victim and make them more vulnerable.

Others are never good enough, weird, or unremarkable.

Whereas narcissists are brilliant, special, and very interesting.

Compliments are an acknowledgement of other people's qualities and a threat to the superior position of the narcissist. Therefore, it suits them to put others down.

It is a safety mechanism.

Your narcissist is very critical of others and is looking to influence you.

They want you to collude with them and try to indoctrinate you.

It is difficult to stay neutral when the negativity about others is constantly pointed out.

Your narcissist is hoping for a breakdown of your connections with friends, family, colleagues, and others.

When your narcissist is critical, just step away and make up your own mind.

Don't share your appreciation about others with them either.

Sneering remark from narcissistic partner:

'So you call yourself a psychotherapist and you can't even explain to me what's wrong? What a useless professional you are.'

RULEBOOK OF A NARCISSIST
17

I create drama to ensure that I am centre stage

Narcissists aim to be the centre of attention and for that reason they don't like funerals or weddings (unless it is their own).

Funerals are often not attended and at weddings they manage to attract attention through creating drama.

Being late (Rule 8 'I make everyone wait for me')

Having a loud argument.

Shouting and running up the stairs.

Falling on the floor in tears.

Having a (fake) heart attack.

Anything.

As long as it puts them centre stage.

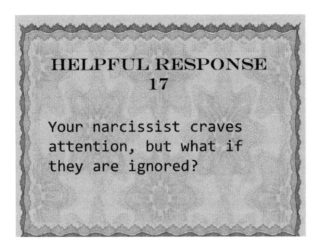

**HELPFUL RESPONSE
17**

Your narcissist craves attention, but what if they are ignored?

You know your narcissist wants to be noticed.

The best position for them is when everyone pays attention to them.

That's why they create drama in the first place.

The best response is to ignore their drama and get on with what you are doing.

This can spark anger in your narcissist, and they might change their focus from the drama towards punishing you. As you are disloyal to them (their thinking pattern is you are against them) and seem to have a good time, Rule 52 'If I can't have it, you can't have it either' comes into play. I always suggest you prepare yourself for these events, by informing a few friends, who might protect and support you.

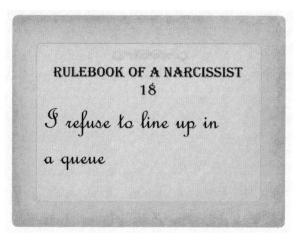

RULEBOOK OF A NARCISSIST
18

I refuse to line up in

a queue

Narcissists couldn't possibly lower themselves to the level of the 'common public' and be treated as everybody else. Especially not when it comes to queueing.

Waiting in a line means there is no control. They just have to follow what happens to them and all the others.

They tend to walk straight to the front (I have seen it happen at airports and ski lifts), pushing people out of the way and just bashing through.

It is surprising how often they get away with it.

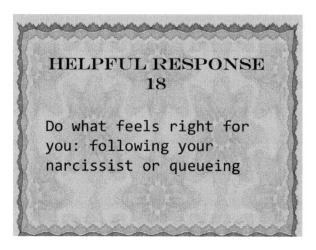

HELPFUL RESPONSE
18

Do what feels right for
you: following your
narcissist or queueing

It can be very embarrassing to be put in a position where you feel forced to violate your values, such as respect, in order to 'support' your narcissist's behaviour. Or to take the risk of a massive argument by not colluding with them.

You have free will.

But there are always consequences of your choice.

One of the difficulties in the relationship with your narcissist is that you are pressurised to contradict what is important to you. It causes an internal battle.

How far are you removed from yourself?

RULEBOOK OF A NARCISSIST
19

I will never forget anything I can use against someone else

Narcissists are walking databases with an incredibly huge hard drive. They collect information from other people, store it and get it out when they can use it to embarrass someone, put them down or disgrace them.

Something that a 20-year-old tells them might be held against them when they are 40.

When narcissists wear their mask, they are charming and chatty, on a mission not just to make a great impression but also to gather data.

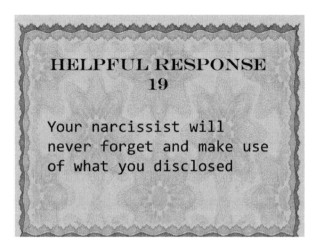

HELPFUL RESPONSE
19

Your narcissist will
never forget and make use
of what you disclosed

Be careful what you share with your narcissist.

Financial information, pin codes, old trauma's, situations you felt vulnerable, little mistakes you regret, it will all be kept in your narcissist's head.

To be used when it suits them to diminish you.

Behind closed doors.

In front of your friends.

To embarrass you in public.

Don't be open with your narcissist. It can only harm you.

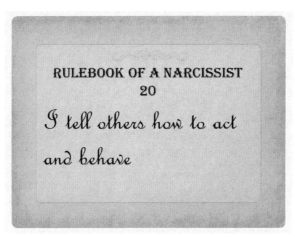

RULEBOOK OF A NARCISSIST
20

I tell others how to act

and behave

Narcissists always know better, even in situations where it is not relevant, or appropriate.

They bully and bark. They will tell the waiter to write the order down. They will discuss in the supermarket how lousy the checkout system is and they will shout at personal trainers in the gym that they got it wrong.

It is underlining their importance, even though the context might be totally inappropriate.

It is one of those typical situations where your narcissist winds themselves up to prove the point that they are better.

It will not be possible to discuss their behaviour with them (Rule 1 'I am better than anybody else' and Rule 2 'I am perfect') and the best thing is to detach yourself.

You are not responsible for the behaviour of your narcissist.

Often, it is best to step aside and disengage.

My narcissist brother always gives me orders. He takes the lead, telling me what to do.

"Ring funeral directors, organise email invitations, inform all of death. Do not approve coffin, hymns or wake without speaking to me first."

> ## RULEBOOK OF A NARCISSIST
> ## 21
>
> *I choose a profession that gives me status*

Narcissists choose professions that give them status, power, control, and money. You will find quite a few of them in politics, committees, science, the medical profession, and dentistry.

Charity work is done to look good to the outside world and not because they support the cause or want to make the world a better place.

This rule is connected with the value of image and appearance.

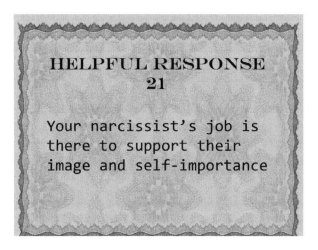

**HELPFUL RESPONSE
21**

Your narcissist's job is
there to support their
image and self-importance

It is your job to let your narcissist know that you admire them for their job. Also, that their job is always more credible and important than yours.

Knowing this means you can give your narcissist what they want and avoid unpleasant confrontations.

'Fluffing up your narcissist' will positively affect their mood and your chances of some peace.

Speaking your mind to your narcissist doesn't serve you.

Unfortunately.

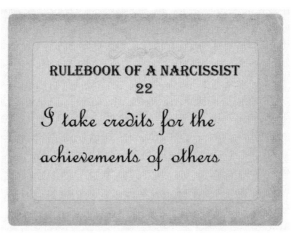

RULEBOOK OF A NARCISSIST
22

I take credits for the achievements of others

Narcissists will show off, claiming it was them who had the idea or did the work.

They will take photos and create social media posts, pretending they accomplished the results. Even though they might have nothing to do with it.

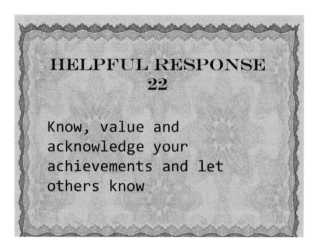

HELPFUL RESPONSE
22

Know, value and
acknowledge your
achievements and let
others know

Your narcissist will take the credits for your success and attainments.

They are naturally jealous of other people's success.

It is important that you own your achievements because your narcissist will try to claim that the success is theirs.

Don't challenge your narcissist openly but do let other people know the truth. It is like running your own campaign, to be seen for who you really are.

While his mother designed her son's garden and worked two weeks to get it ready for him, he posted photos pretending he had done it all himself.

No credits for his mum.

I am always campaigning to get people in my tribe

In order to gain support to control and manipulate activities, narcissists are constantly lobbying to get people on their side. This is important as their thought pattern of 'You are either with me or against me', divides the world into two types of people. The people who are with them need to prove their commitment by supporting smear campaigns, doing 'investigations' or acting on their behalf.

The people in their tribe are called 'flying monkeys'.

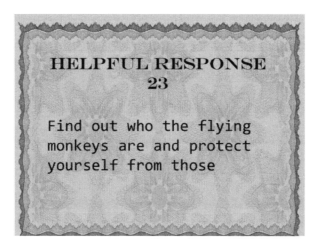

**HELPFUL RESPONSE
23**

Find out who the flying
monkeys are and protect
yourself from those

Your narcissist will use the flying monkeys to get more control over you. If you know who they are, you can protect yourself from their invasion. To avoid the manipulation of the flying monkeys, be aware of events that don't feel right or genuine. They might invite you or being overly friendly, trying to get information. They are secretly acting on behalf of your narcissist to manipulate you.

Keep yourself safe from their influence by knowing who the flying monkeys are and what their purpose is.

Rule series 2

All about you, my target, my victim

I take control of you, your feelings, behaviour and of course, I know best as I am perfect.

A lot of these rule are projections: ideas and feelings that I have about myself but can't admit or deal with. Instead, I will attribute these to others.

24   You are sooooo stupid, useless and horrible

25   You get it wrong all the time

26   You are always so negative

27   No one believes you

28   You always ruin everything

29   Everybody else thinks that you are awful

30   You are a taker

31   I know how you feel and think, better than you do yourself

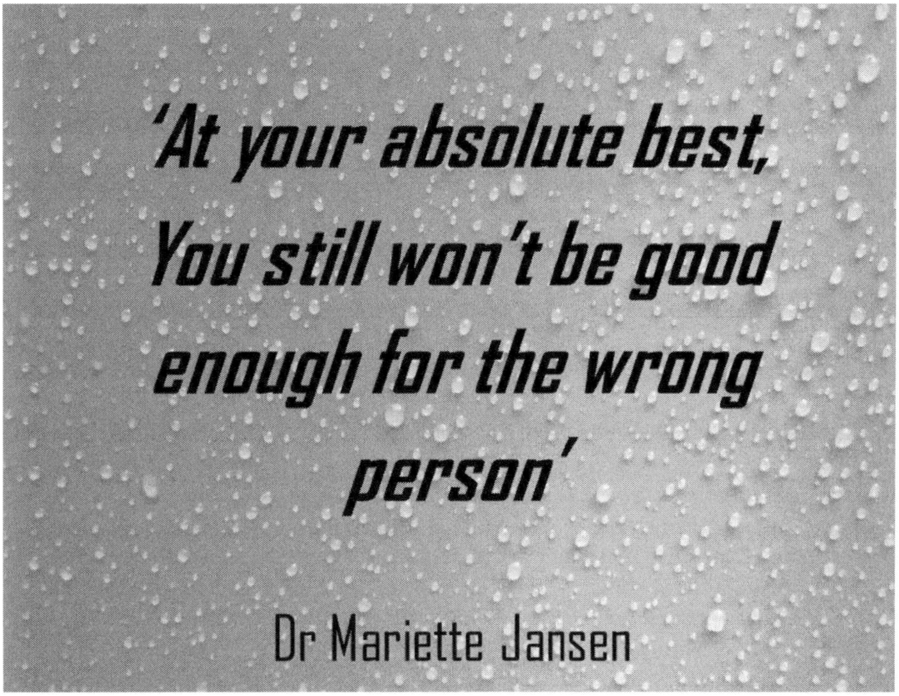

'At your absolute best,
You still won't be good
enough for the wrong
person'

Dr Mariette Jansen

RULEBOOK OF A NARCISSIST
24

You are sooooo stupid,
useless and horrible

Narcissists easily throw out devaluing comments towards their victims.

Often when they are angry, don't get their way or are just feeling moody.

They make sure the message is communicated through words, sounds and body language.

Imagine a dismissive tone of voice and the facial expression of disgust.

Their black and white thinking results in these absolute statements and can leave their victims deeply hurt.

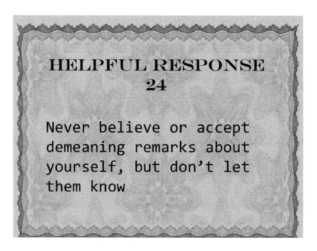

**HELPFUL RESPONSE
24**

Never believe or accept
demeaning remarks about
yourself, but don't let
them know

Your narcissist is denigrating you in order to ensure their position is at the top.

They need internal confirmation that they are above you and get that by putting you down. It is a technique that is applied by the weak, and insecure.

Don't pay attention or engage with comments like this.

Don't take them seriously.

Never doubt yourself.

You are beautiful, unique, and special in your own right.

There is a diamond inside you.

Don't let the diamond lose its shine.

Your narcissist doesn't want you to shine, as you might outshine them.

They just vent their frustration on you, and it is important for your mental health to learn to shake it off.

RULEBOOK OF A NARCISSIST
25

You get it wrong all the time

Narcissists like to speak in absolutes.

And telling someone they get it wrong 'all the time' is an example.

It demonstrates how they think in black and white.

It is also an easy way to sow seeds of doubt within someone else.

It is part of the gaslighting process, aiming to confuse and undermine confidence.

> ## HELPFUL RESPONSE
> ## 25
>
> You don't get it wrong
> all the time. Everyone
> gets it wrong some of the
> time, even your
> narcissist

Your narcissist is talking to you like this to present themselves with unsubstantiated authority.

It is serving them as it makes them feel good about themselves. It aims to make you feel insecure.

It is pre-empting anything you say and making sure that nothing needs to be taken seriously.

After all, 'you always get it wrong'.

You know it isn't true.

Don't believe it.

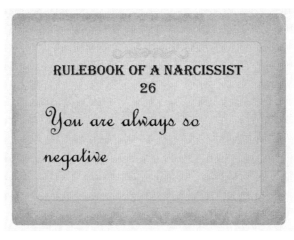

RULEBOOK OF A NARCISSIST
26

You are always so negative

Narcissists struggle to live with a light and positive outlook.

Life for them is hard, as they can't ever let go of their protection mechanisms.

They need to be on the lookout for danger to keep themselves safe at all times.

No wonder that for them life isn't an easy ride.

As a result, most narcissists have a really negative attitude.

They are always coming from the dark side.

Telling others that they are negative is a typical projection of their own state of mind.

And this accusation often evokes a defence ('No, I am not negative'), which put the narcissist in the authoritarian position.

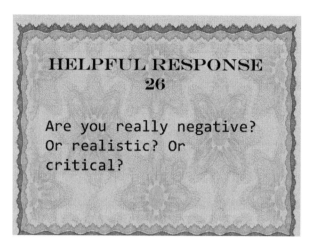

**HELPFUL RESPONSE
26**

Are you really negative?
Or realistic? Or
critical?

Your narcissist wants you to feel bad about yourself.

When you are critical, you are negative.

When you want to discuss a situation but they won't, you are negative.

When you have the courage to challenge them, you are negative.

Being negative is a way to bring the focus back to you and what you are doing wrong.

It is a deflection from the content of your message to your 'wrongdoing'.

Recognise your intention, recognise their projection, and know your narcissist is blaming you to keep themselves safe.

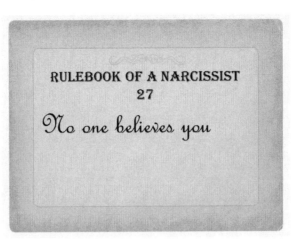

RULEBOOK OF A NARCISSIST
27

No one believes you

Narcissists wear a mask of charm and kindness when they meet other people.

Others get to know them as the life and soul of a party, the person who is generous and buys the drinks, the one who is concerned about their (victim) partner.

Their image and appearance in the outside world is very different than their behaviour in the 'safe' environment at home, behind closed doors.

That is where they show their manipulation and nastiness and only their victims know.

When a victim speaks out about the narcissistic abuse, it confuses others, who have this very different, positive impression.

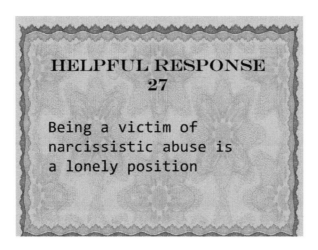

**HELPFUL RESPONSE
27**

Being a victim of
narcissistic abuse is
a lonely position

The game your narcissist plays is all about them taking control of their image, which is an important value to them. They need to be perceived as a great person and present that mask of grandiosity, generosity, and gentleness. Their false persona.

You know the real person, behind the mask.

The controller, who not only controls you but also the people you know by portraying themselves in different manners: kind and fun to others, cruel and negative to you.

It might be difficult to find people to talk to, as people will struggle with the different images of your narcissist.

Before you confide, dip your toe in the water with someone to gauge their reaction.

If they don't believe you, leave it.

If they are open to listen and not judge, dip in another toe.

And slowly open up, all the way gauging their feedback and support.

'Well, this relationship
didn't work out.
And it is you.
It is certainly not me.'

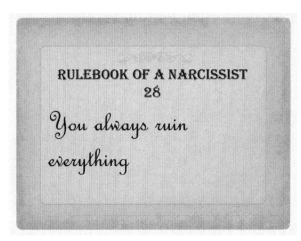

RULEBOOK OF A NARCISSIST
28

You always ruin everything

Narcissists never take responsibility and present themselves as the victim when something doesn't go according to plan.

They brainwash their victim into believing that it was their fault.

Victims of narcissists over time are conditioned into taking the blame and feeling the responsibility, believing they ruin 'our family, your family, your friends, my work, holidays, fun nights out, everything'.

Notice the use of absolutes: always and everything.

It is their black and white thinking that doesn't leave any space for the in-between.

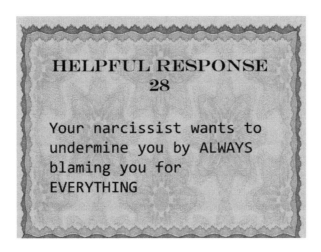

**HELPFUL RESPONSE
28**

Your narcissist wants to
undermine you by ALWAYS
blaming you for
EVERYTHING

Your narcissist wants to indoctrinate you with the thought that you always get it wrong.

Over time, it will become so ingrained in your way of thinking that you will automatically ponder: 'What mistake did I make? Is it my fault?' Not only in situations with your narcissist, but in any situation.

Your narcissist will tell you that they suffer ('poor me') as a result of your failings.

To make you feel even worse.

They fuel your feeling of Fear ('What if I don't comply?'), Obligation ('I owe them this') and Guilt ('I made a mistake').

It's called FOG.

Consider how FOG is clouding your judgement and undermining your confidence.

Challenge yourself by asking the question: 'Is what you are being accused of by your narcissist really true?'

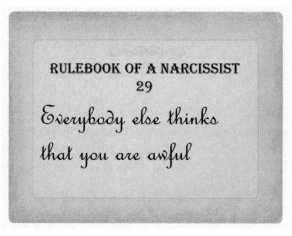

RULEBOOK OF A NARCISSIST
29
Everybody else thinks that you are awful

Narcissists love talking on behalf of others and about others.

Gossiping is a word that springs to mind, especially the nasty, smearing kind.

Smearing is spreading awful and untrue stories about someone else, with the aim to put them in a bad light.

When people are bonding and building strong connections, it forms a threat for narcissists as it diminishes the success of their favourite relationship game: 'divide and rule' or 'divide and conquer'.

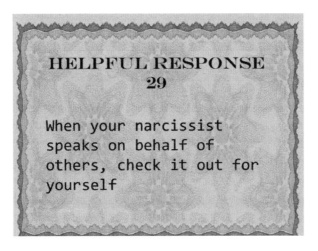

HELPFUL RESPONSE
29

When your narcissist
speaks on behalf of
others, check it out for
yourself

Often you will find that your narcissist has made up what was said for a variety of reasons.

First of all, to upset and manipulate you.

Secondly, to disturb the relationship you have with others.

Your narcissist aims to alienate you from others, as this makes you an easier target for them.

Your narcissist is jealous and fearful of the influence of other people in your life.

Thirdly, to create a 'bad' image of you, so people will indeed think you are awful.

The smearing usually becomes stronger when the relationship with your narcissist dwindles, aiming to make you weaker and them stronger.

Be prepared to be exposed to smearing and make sure you keep a few trusted friends or family members in your circle.

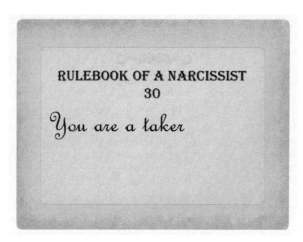

RULEBOOK OF A NARCISSIST
30
You are a taker

Most narcissists are keen on money and are prepared to work hard to get it.

They are often successful managers, salespeople, traders, businesspeople, or high-profile politicians and professionals.

Once they have established their success and reel in the money, they are thriving.

Wealth is a value for them and a tool to ensure their status.

It is the external validation of their 'specialness'.

They will also use money as a power tool to control and reward 'good' behaviour.

And to induce guilt for spending money that is earned by them.

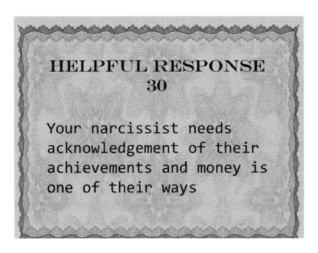

HELPFUL RESPONSE
30

Your narcissist needs
acknowledgement of their
achievements and money is
one of their ways

In healthy relationships, it is about sharing and looking after each other.

Often there is one partner who will bring in more money, but it is to be enjoyed by all.

Everyone plays their part and contributes.

Be it with money, time, attention, or love.

Your narcissist uses money as a way to present themselves as better than the rest and a tool to control.

If you are in a position where you don't have a choice but accept their money, be aware it will be used against you.

If you are in a position where you have a choice, choose wisely.

Always make sure you have some money set aside, that way you are not totally dependent on your narcissist.

Look how hard I worked

Look at my success

Look at the money I brought in

Look at you

What do you have to show for?

Apart from spending my money

User

Parasite

Leech

> **RULEBOOK OF A NARCISSIST**
> **31**
>
> *I know how you feel and think, better than you do yourself*

Narcissists take control of the feelings and thoughts of their victims.

Just by telling them constantly what they (should) feel or think.

'I am angry.'

'No, you are not, you are spoilt.'

'I am upset.'

'No, you are not. You are oversensitive.'

It is an attempt to make their victims question themselves and confuse them. It is a form of gaslighting (making someone doubt their own reality by continuously disagreeing with or confusing them) and creating a huge insecurity.

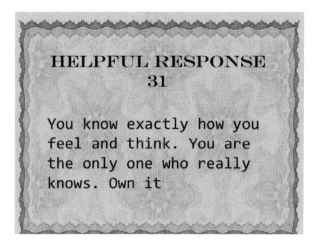

**HELPFUL RESPONSE
31**

You know exactly how you
feel and think. You are
the only one who really
knows. Own it

Your narcissist wants you to doubt yourself and is continuously campaigning.

Why?

It is easier to control someone who feels insecure and questions themselves, then someone who is certain and might question them back.

You know yourself, your thoughts, and your feelings.

It is important to stay true to yourself and trust your gut feeling.

No one knows what someone else feels or thinks. Only the one who is thinking and feeling knows what is going on.

Record events, conversations, and situations to remind yourself of how you feel and think.

This will help you to check and trust your recollection and memories.

Rule series 3

All about me controlling you

This is where I reprimand and bully you. I will tell you what to do and how I think you should behave. I want to control everything about you to suit my needs.

32 You deserve punishment: silent treatment, changing plans or cancelling events

33 How dare you speak to me like that?

34 You don't even understand what you did wrong?

35 Stop putting me under pressure, pushing me or being needy

36 I would never put you down, I am just telling how it is

37 It is really difficult to love you

38 Stop criticising, challenging, judging and disapproving

39 You were flirting, you are having an affair

40   Stop being opinionated and outspoken

41   How could you say or even think something like that about me?

42   You need to change

My boyfriend always confused me.

Let's talk openly. I want to know your feelings.

Then I opened up and told him what I felt.

He then said he totally got it, as he felt the same.

And continued talking on about himself.

Any conversation always was about him.

RULEBOOK OF A NARCISSIST
32

You deserve punishment:
silent treatment, changing
plans or cancelling events

Narcissists get angry with people who are acting 'against' them or not complying.

Acting against them means acting differently from what they want or prioritising something or somebody else over them.

In other words, they feel threatened and insecure. This is unacceptable and means punishment is on the agenda.

The silent treatment, which can last for weeks, is extremely effective as their victims are usually empathic people who seek to sort conflicts and create peace.

Taking control of plans and events is another way of showing their superiority over someone who dared to disobey or disagree.

**HELPFUL RESPONSE
32**

Punishment is
unacceptable in a
respectful relationship

Your narcissist doesn't show any respect for you when they think it is okay to punish you.

You are both adults.

At least that is the idea.

But your narcissist behaves like a toddler who is angry with you and acts out.

Changing plans or cancelling events, shows that you have no say in these matters.

It demonstrates the imbalance of power.

The silent treatment aims to make you feel uncomfortable, insecure, restless and nervous. And hopefully makes you beg your narcissist to end it.

It is very difficult to find a healthy response to these punishments, as they are disrespectful towards you and are aimed to show who has the power.

Is this a relationship that makes you happy?

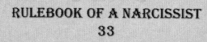

RULEBOOK OF A NARCISSIST
33

How dare you speak to me like that?

Narcissists will manipulate communication, changing the focus from content to process.

From 'what you are saying' to 'how you say it'.

They deter from the original focus, which might be critical of them, and direct the emphasis on someone else's faults.

'Why are you so grumpy?'

'Oh no, here we go again. Being negative and critical. Can't you ever talk about something nice?'

Changing the focus is one of their regularly used manipulation techniques.

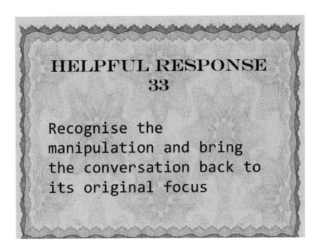

**HELPFUL RESPONSE
33**

Recognise the
manipulation and bring
the conversation back to
its original focus

Explaining situations or feelings to your narcissist is always a challenge.

If your narcissist thinks you are critical, they will change the focus away from the content of your message and no matter how many different ways you try to get it across, it will never land.

Noticing the change of focus will help you to protect yourself from the desperation of feeling misunderstood and not heard.

Once you have tried twice to deliver your content to the deaf ears of your narcissist, you might as well give up and accept that they are not willing to hear you.

RULEBOOK OF A NARCISSIST
34

You don't even understand what you did wrong?

Narcissists have different ways of sarcastically voicing the message that others are stupid. One of them is using a statement like the above, suggestive and vague. It makes people wonder.

'Did I do something wrong? I didn't think I did, but now it is pointed out to me, maybe I might have done. How come I don't understand it?'

It is an effective way to make others doubt themselves. It is a natural reaction, which works in favour of the aim to control someone's mental and emotional space.

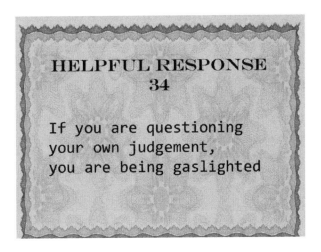

**HELPFUL RESPONSE
34**

If you are questioning
your own judgement,
you are being gaslighted

Gaslighting is a technique where you are manipulated into doubting your own reality.

It works through being continuously challenged about what you say and think.

You start questioning your own judgment, wondering who is right.

Then you start to doubt yourself and believe the one who is right is your narcissist.

When your narcissist demeans you but doesn't bother to explain, don't spend time overthinking.

You are being manipulated.

The little boy was summoned to the office for a talk with his mother, who told him that she wasn't happy with his behaviour. He asked what it was about and she answered that if he didn't know that, he should go to his room and think about it.

He went to his room, desperate to find an answer, ruminating over all what he said and did for the last few days. It left him devastated, as he didn't have any idea what his mother was talking about.

This was one of the ways his mum made sure she was at the forefront of his mind.

RULEBOOK OF A NARCISSIST
35

Stop putting me under pressure, pushing me or being needy

Psychological projection is a defence mechanism often used by narcissists. It involves projecting feelings or emotions they don't like in themselves onto someone else.

Narcissists will accuse their victims of their misconducts.

They put their victims under pressure and push them because they are needy.

They want their supply.

But instead of admitting that, they accuse their victims.

Control and disrespect shine through in this rule.

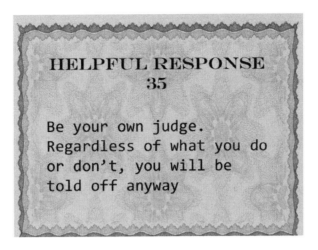

HELPFUL RESPONSE
35

Be your own judge.
Regardless of what you do
or don't, you will be
told off anyway

It is helpful to notice the projection and know that your narcissist is talking about themselves.

Not about you.

Don't be tempted into a discussion.

This is not about you.

Be your own judge, know your own truth.

Try to be a slippery grey rock and let it all slide off you.

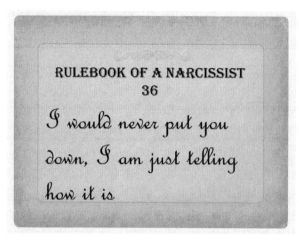

RULEBOOK OF A NARCISSIST
36

I would never put you down, I am just telling how it is

Narcissists love 'word games' and indirect delivery through voice, facial expression and body language.

When challenged, they will say they didn't say anything wrong.

They have a range of ways to put someone down by 'telling' the truth.

'How often do I need to tell you the same thing?'

'You never understand what I mean.'

'Is that going wrong again?'

They use suggestive communication to create upset in their victim but can't be accused of doing something unpleasant as taken literally, they didn't say anything wrong.

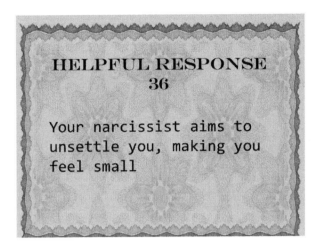

**HELPFUL RESPONSE
36**

Your narcissist aims to
unsettle you, making you
feel small

Your narcissist needs to ensure that your confidence is constantly reducing.

Suggestive, sarcastic (they might say it's a joke) and diminishing (they might say it's a fact) remarks are made to put you in your place.

That place is always beneath them.

The aim of these remarks is to keep chipping away your confidence and sense of self.

You will never be able to challenge your narcissist. They will throw back at you that they haven't said anything wrong.

It is very toxic to be on the receiving end of these type of comments.

The best way of dealing with this is to not engage.

'What did you do to your hair?'
'I let it go grey.'
'Why?'
'Because it's my hair and I am fed
up with colouring it.'
'But now people will think you're your
husband's mother instead of his wife.'

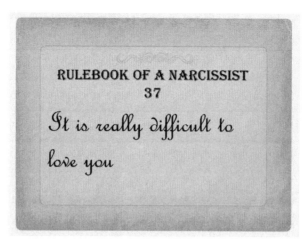

RULEBOOK OF A NARCISSIST
37

It is really difficult to love you

Narcissists create co-dependent relationships, where their victims believe they can't function on their own.

When a victim starts living through their narcissist, thinking on their behalf and making decisions that will benefit the narcissist instead of themselves, the narcissist has all the control.

Exactly what they like.

A romantic partner is a trophy to add to their superiority, an insurance policy for Narcissistic Supply and a source to play the victim card and attract sympathy and attention from others.

To tease their victims and keep them on their toes, they offer opposite messages, such as 'You are my soulmate' and 'It is difficult to love you'.

This often results in the partner working even harder to please the narcissist.

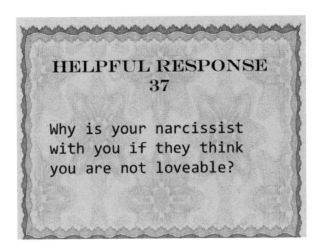

**HELPFUL RESPONSE
37**

Why is your narcissist
with you if they think
you are not loveable?

Bringing you down is one of the techniques your narcissist applies to undermine your confidence:

+ They aim to break you, thinking less of yourself and therefore appreciating them more.

+ Doing more to keep them happy.

+ Trying harder to get their validation.

+ And in that process, losing yourself, your self-esteem and self-worth.

Your narcissist doesn't love you.

They love what you do for them.

That's all.

RULEBOOK OF A NARCISSIST
38

Stop criticising, challenging, judging and disapproving

Narcissists have long toes – it is easy to tread on them.

Any suspicion of a critical word towards them or their actions upsets them.

They are highly critical of others, but that is not relevant.

They are scared to be criticised as this makes them feel vulnerable.

Will they be unmasked?

Is their fragile ego being discovered?

Even remarks that are not meant to be a criticism, challenge, judgment, or disapproval will easily be viewed this way.

Sparking reactions such as anger, dismissal and of course projection, based on the thinking pattern where people are with or against them.

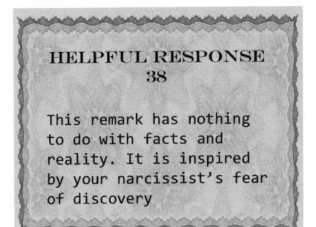

HELPFUL RESPONSE
38

This remark has nothing to do with facts and reality. It is inspired by your narcissist's fear of discovery

Your narcissist is continuously on the lookout for the dangers that jeopardise their image and appearance. It is one of their main values and it is what they work and live for.

Anything that could potentially damage their image needs to be stopped.

A perceived criticism can send them into a narcissistic rage or inspire a punishment.

Even if you don't criticise, challenge, judge or disapprove, they will still accuse you.

It is impossible to have a proper reply, apart from letting it go.

Remember, this is not about you, this is all about them.

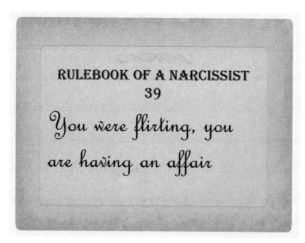

RULEBOOK OF A NARCISSIST
39

You were flirting, you are having an affair

Projection and fear are behind this accusation.

Narcissists are always on the lookout for more Narcissistic Supply and flirting is an easy way to get that. They are known for their infidelity and can have multiple affairs on the go.

If they were subjected to adultery, it would break them. It would be seen as a rejection of their grandiosity and specialness, and it is unacceptable that their partner would prefer someone else over them.

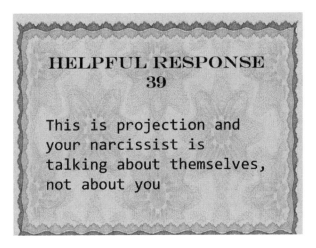

**HELPFUL RESPONSE
39**

This is projection and
your narcissist is
talking about themselves,
not about you

Unfair accusations make you defend yourself and explain that whatever your narcissist thought is not true.

You are eager to prove your point.

However, your narcissist is convinced and whatever you say will not change their mind.

Their jealousy is sparked by their insecurity, not by your behaviour.

Their accusation is a form of projection.

You know your truth, don't let the delusion of your narcissist get to you.

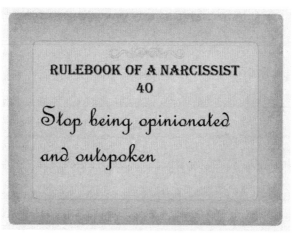

RULEBOOK OF A NARCISSIST
40

Stop being opinionated and outspoken

Narcissists are not keen on people with strong opposing opinions.

Opinions are only appreciated when they support the narcissist.

Anyone who dares to have a different opinion is damned.

Simple, black and white thinking.

And the idea of 'you are either with me or against me' means that thinking differently is a token of war: 'You are against me'.

When first meeting people, narcissists will check out how opiniated someone else is and if they are, it is curtains for them.

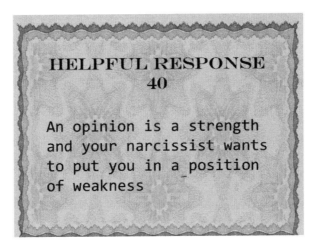

**HELPFUL RESPONSE
40**

An opinion is a strength
and your narcissist wants
to put you in a position
of weakness

Your narcissist wants you to be 'with them', not 'against them', and a different opinion is the sign of a strong person who dares to challenge them.

It means you are against them.

They can't separate an opinion on a subject from an opinion about themselves.

An opposing outlook is felt as a personal attack.

Have you lost your opinion since being with your narcissistic partner?

As a child of a narcissistic parent, have you ever developed an opinion?

If you notice it is hard to think independently, it is a sign of emotional abuse.

RULEBOOK OF A NARCISSIST
41

How could you even think something like that about me?

Narcissists are easily offended.

If someone says something that could be taken as offensive, they will manipulate the context and blame, accuse or playing the guilt card.

Or act like a victim. 'Poor me', 'Look what you are doing to me', trying to feed the guilt.

Or sharing how 'disappointed' they are in the other person.

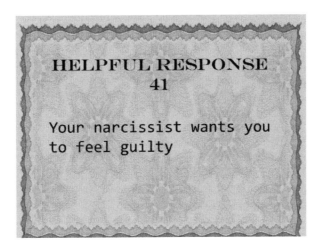

**HELPFUL RESPONSE
41**

Your narcissist wants you
to feel guilty

An innocent remark or question will be put in a different context by your narcissist, who wants you to feel you did something wrong. That is certainly what you want to avoid because doing something wrong never pays off as your narcissist will punish you (Rule 32 'You deserve punishment: silent treatment, changing plans or cancelling events').

Your narcissist pushes you into a defensive position. You most likely feel the need to explain that you didn't mean it like it. But your narcissist will point out how badly you behaved.

It is important to recognise the manipulation, not defend yourself, and if relevant, bring the conversation back to the content of the original message.

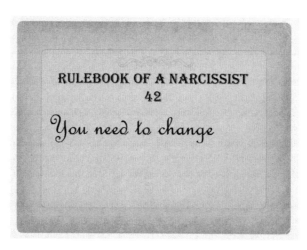

RULEBOOK OF A NARCISSIST
42
You need to change

Narcissists are quick to point the finger at others, and if things don't happen the way they want, it is others who need to change.

Never them.

After all, they are perfect.

Often, they are vague about what exactly needs to be changed.

Keeping it unclear adds to the confusion of their victims, who don't know what is expected of them.

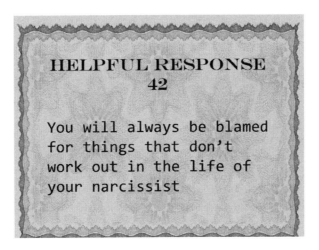

HELPFUL RESPONSE
42

You will always be blamed
for things that don't
work out in the life of
your narcissist

Your narcissist will never take responsibility when things go wrong.

Blaming you when things aren't going the way they want.

They are quick taking the credit when things go right though.

You need to be true to yourself and avoid taking on board the idea that it is your fault and that it is you who needs to make amendments.

It makes sense to ask your narcissist exactly what needs to be changed and how. Often they won't be able to answer and will throw it back at you: 'You mean you don't know? You don't even get this?' Hoping to confuse you even more and feeding your sense of incompetence and guilt.

If your narcissist isn't able to tell you what they want you to change, just let it go.

'I want you to change.'
'What do you want me to change?'
'I don't know.'
'Well, in that case there is nothing I can do.'

Rule series 4

All about how I want
the relationship to work

I set the rules, you follow.

I tell you what I want, and you obey.

This is my textbook on how we relate, and I dictate.

43   You have to make it happen for me into certain actions. But does this feel right?

44   You are lucky to have me, no one else would put up with

45   It is an honour to serve me

46   I will always get what I want

47   I am the best you will ever get

48   No one can be trusted, but me

49   I decide for you

50   I will pester you until you give in

51   Stop being you, be me

52   If I can't have it, you can't have it either

53   We have the best relationship in the world. Everybody envies us

54   I mirror and copy your behaviour, text messages and ideas

55   I might leave you or I might give you another chance?

56   I take up most of your mental space

57   Our relationship is conditional. If you obey me, I will accept you

58   If that makes you happy, I will take it away

59   Your behaviour sparks my behaviour. If you don't like mine, change yours

60   Look how much I am doing for you

61   I move the goalposts whenever it suits me

62   When I compliment you, there is always a sting

63   You are my toy, I play with you like a cat plays with a mouse

Narcissists don't love people,

they only love

what people have to offer

Dr Mariette Jansen

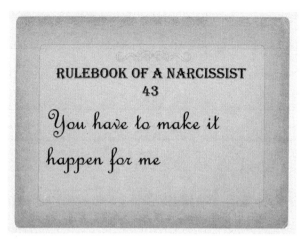

RULEBOOK OF A NARCISSIST
43

You have to make it happen for me

Narcissists like to make others responsible for what they want to happen.

As a parent they might say to their partner: 'Make the children talk to me' or 'Let them behave differently'.

As a partner they might say that life is boring, 'You have to bring some excitement in'.

This is where narcissists bring in a co-dependent element, merging two individuals into one.

They will take a backseat and expect others to arrange and organise what they want.

It is not for them to take action, initiative or responsibility.

They are the directors, dictating others how to act. This is for their both their victims and flying monkeys (Rule 23 'I am campaigning to get people in my tribe').

Your narcissist tries to force you to act on their behalf to create what they desire.

You may see it as important for you to give your narcissist what they want in order to keep the peace and because 'it is no big deal', or because you believe you should have made it happen in the first place.

If you are making excuses for your narcissist, it is as if you take responsibility for their behaviour. That is a sign of co-dependency.

Ask yourself if it is okay that you are made solely responsible and then decide what to do.

RULEBOOK OF A NARCISSIST
44

You are lucky to have me, no one else would put up with you

Narcissists keep on repeating devaluing messages to their victims. This works two ways: lifting themselves up, while putting others down.

It is their way of making themselves special. As if they are a winning ticket in the lottery. It shows their need to be valued and put on a pedestal and clearly

emphasises the imbalance in the relationship.

It is also an attempt to keep the relationship going, through undermining the confidence of their victim.

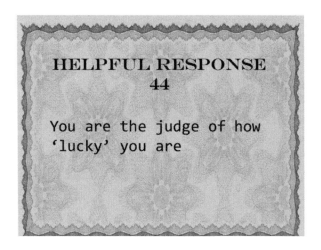

HELPFUL RESPONSE
44

You are the judge of how 'lucky' you are

Narcissists love to make it seems like they have rescued you. It creates an unhealthy connection where you seem to be depending on your narcissist. This is called co-dependency.

Instead of you being independent, a person in your own right, your narcissist wants you to feel that you needed to be saved. Consider your 'lucky' moments. How often does your narcissist make you feel happy?

The position of rescuer elevates them above you and will put you in a position of owing them.

Unfortunately, you will never be saved by or safe in the company of a narcissist. To find answers, start documenting facts about what is happening in your relationship and then consider your 'luck'.

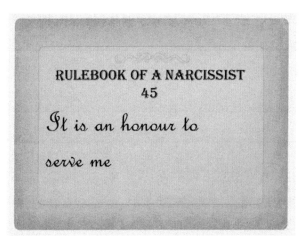

RULEBOOK OF A NARCISSIST
45

It is an honour to serve me

Narcissists have a strong sense of entitlement. They take for granted that other people will do tasks for them, help them out and support them. This should be seen by their victims as a privilege. Over time, the demands often become so huge that victims feel treated like they are being a slave.

An unspoken rule in the romantic relationship is that the victim should feel privileged to be the chosen one and has to 'reward' the narcissist (Rule 44 'You are lucky to have me, no one else would put up with you').

Narcissists won't thank others for what they do and won't show appreciation.

When people have had enough and stop serving, narcissists will drop them without a second thought and look for replacements.

There will be no appreciation, only dismissiveness. And forget about loyalty.

Your narcissist wants to make you think you are obliged to run their errands and look after their needs. After all, they deserve this because of who they are.

Your narcissist will apply FOG: forcing you into serving through Fear, talking about Obligation and playing the Guilt card.

You won't get a 'thank you' or a 'well done' as you are seen as a servant and beneath them. However, servants get paid for doing their jobs. Do you?

Your life is not about serving your narcissist, your life is about finding yourself, serving yourself and taking care of you.

Are you aware of your reasons for serving your narcissist? How much is induced by fear, obligation, or guilt?

If you know your reasons and they are around FOG, you are ready to leave your narcissist and serve yourself.

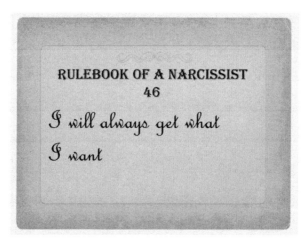

RULEBOOK OF A NARCISSIST
46

I will always get what I want

Narcissists are focused and single-minded.

They won't take no for an answer.

The thought that prevails here is that there are only winners and losers and therefore 'I need to win'. They won't give up and will go to any length and effort to win. There is a serious threat here. Their lack of empathy, love of Schadenfreude (Rule 5 'I thrive on the misery of others') and value of self-importance can lead to actions that damage their victims.

It is one of the reasons that makes divorcing a narcissist a very painful experience.

This rule also makes them great salespeople and successful but unpopular managers.

Their life is about winning.

```
HELPFUL RESPONSE
46

This is a serious threat
and you need to be
prepared that your
narcissist will never
give up
```

Often you might give in to your narcissist.

For the sake of peace.

For your own sense of calm.

These battles can take years and will only end when your narcissist gets what they want.

If you are divorcing your narcissist or taking 'no contact' approach, make sure you prepare on all practical, legal, and financial levels.

Involve professionals to support you and be prepared for a tough ride.

Text message exchange

I need to talk to you today, just 15 minutes.

Sorry I don't have time.

Everyone can find 15 minutes.

You are not the PM.

CALL ME NOW

I AM CALLING YOU NOW

PICK UP THE BLOODY PHONE

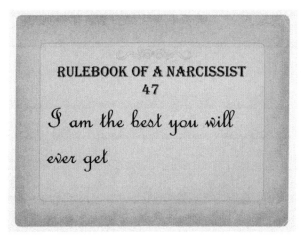

RULEBOOK OF A NARCISSIST
47

I am the best you will ever get

What could be the reason to say this to your partner?

How would it serve the relationship?

Narcissists lift themselves up by putting their partner down and creating a bigger gap between the two of them.

In normal relationships the aim is to get closer to each other.

Narcissists struggle with intimacy and vulnerability and are not able to emotionally connect.

They engage in a romantic relationship to ensure their Narcissistic Supply: attention, admiration, and confirmation.

And to secure the supply, they need to make sure their partner stays. One way is to present themselves as the best, someone to hold onto and to not let go off.

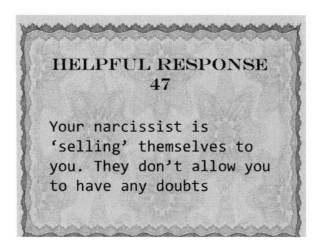

**HELPFUL RESPONSE
47**

Your narcissist is
'selling' themselves to
you. They don't allow you
to have any doubts

Relationships are about balance, respect and equality.

Your narcissist does not support these ideas.

They are keen to create an imbalance by flaunting themselves as the 'better' party and will not show respect for you and your qualities. Your narcissist plants the idea in your head that you have done well to 'catch' them and the fear that you are not good enough to get someone else.

Do you feel fear?

Do you feel unequal?

Remember that your narcissist is insecure and try not to pay attention to this rule, which is intended to make you insecure.

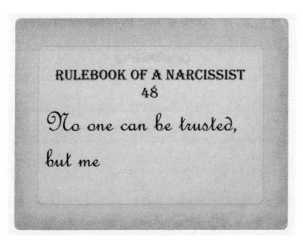

RULEBOOK OF A NARCISSIST
48

No one can be trusted, but me

Narcissists project what is going on within themselves onto the world.

They can't be trusted by others as their values of dishonesty, disloyalty and self-importance will always prevail over caring for others.

They steal if they consider that they should have what someone else possesses (Rule 52 'If I can't have it, you can't have it either').

They lie if reality needs to be adapted.

They twist to suit their agenda.

And then they tell their children, friends or partners that no one can be trusted.

Except for them.

Children raised by narcissistic parents have a low trust threshold and are suspicious for two reasons: deep down they know they can't trust their parents and they have been told they can't trust others.

The 'but me' part is that extra addition to put themselves in higher position and invites their victim to be open and vulnerable, hoping to get more ammunition for abuse.

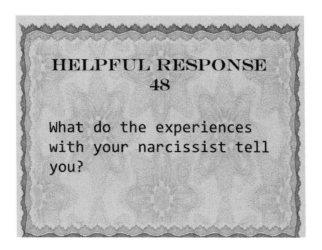

HELPFUL RESPONSE
48

What do the experiences with your narcissist tell you?

Do you feel you can trust your narcissist?

Have they ever betrayed you?

Do they encourage and support you?

Do they always do as they say?

Or are you disappointed with your narcissist?

Walking on eggshells?

Is your narcissist moody and unpredictable?

Do they make up stories and twist the truth?

You can't trust your narcissist.

It's best to not confide in them and always check out what they tell you.

Trust is earned,
respect is given,
loyalty is demonstrated.
Betrayal of any of these means
losing all three.

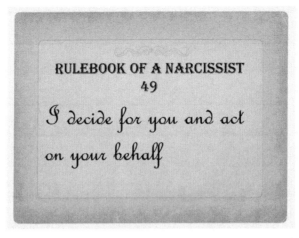

RULEBOOK OF A NARCISSIST
49

I decide for you and act on your behalf

Narcissists take decisions on behalf of their victims as part of their power system. All the choices serve and benefit them and their need to control.

They select what their victims wear, where to go and what to do.

They might disguise their control by pretending they offer their victim a favour, by offering to drive them and pick them up. That way they know where they are and can set the start and end time.

Or they dress it up as an act of support, like doing the shopping together, but only buying what they approve off.

Very much like a dictator, ruling their country and its inhabitants.

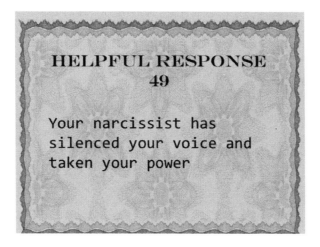

**HELPFUL RESPONSE
49**

Your narcissist has
silenced your voice and
taken your power

It is very disempowering to be in a situation like this.

The perfect relationship for your narcissist is where they call the shots on your behalf and you are supposed to follow without complaining, commenting, or judging.

It is a situation that gives your narcissist total control.

How would it be for you to take some control back?

One way is to manipulate your narcissist by subtly alternating giving in and making your own decisions. You have to be careful as they might get angry and behave in an unpleasant towards you.

Where possible, do your thing: choose what to wear, the time you go out or come back and decide what to eat. Don't allow your narcissist to decide everything for you.

Gently take some control back.

Some people confuse love with control.
Loving someone is letting them be.
Controlling someone is like owning them.

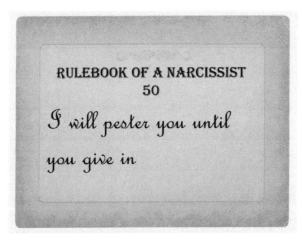

RULEBOOK OF A NARCISSIST
50

I will pester you until you give in

Narcissists need to have their own way.

At any cost.

They will not give in, as their life is about winning.

Winning every situation, battle, or argument.

They pester others until numbness kicks in and giving in is the only way to stop the relentless pestering.

It is down to their thought pattern about winners and losers.

It is unacceptable to them to be seen as a loser.

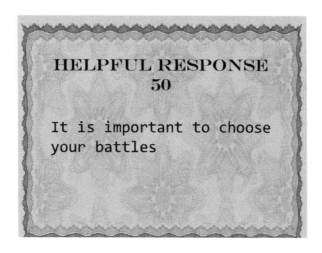

**HELPFUL RESPONSE
50**

It is important to choose
your battles

For your narcissist, every situation in life is about winning.

As they won't stop until they are the victor, it is up to you to decide how to handle these types of situations.

The battle plays out in text messages (10 within an hour), phone calls (at the most inconvenient times) and endless emails (to all your different accounts).

Bombarding you, never allowing you to let it rest.

Until your narcissist feels they have won.

Often, it might be useful to let go of your ego and give in for the sake of peace and space.

Otherwise, it will go on forever.

And forever might mean years.

Your narcissist will remember, and in years to come will still try to win this battle.

Consider how your mental and emotional state are being affected by engaging in the battle and find ways to keep yourself safe and sane.

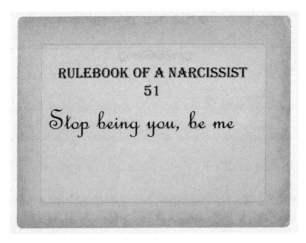

RULEBOOK OF A NARCISSIST
51

Stop being you, be me

Narcissists chose partners they can easily control.

The journey they are taking their partner on is one of breaking them down, then gradually building them up according to their own wishes and requirements.

Narcissists destroy their victim's personalities and then replace them with their own ideas.

There are numerous examples of empathic partners who have been turned into the perfect complimentary adaptation of their narcissist. Complying with the narcissists requirement and teaming up with them to face the outside world.

Often their victims become totally co-dependent, living their lives through them and becoming a narcissist too.

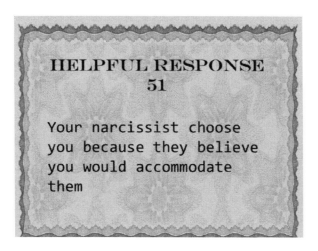

HELPFUL RESPONSE
51

Your narcissist choose
you because they believe
you would accommodate
them

Your narcissist intuitively thought you were easy to mould into how they wanted you to be.

When parts of you are emerging that don't adhere to the requirements of your narcissist they will try to break you down.

If you start to step into your power and be your own person, your narcissist will do everything to bring you back into their way of being, thinking and living.

Your narcissist will occupy your mental space and take over.

How much mental energy do you spend on your narcissist?

How often are they at the forefront of your mind?

The centre of your thoughts?

If you think this is too much, visualise a stop sign. Whenever you notice your narcissist takes over, see the sign, stop and think about something completely different.

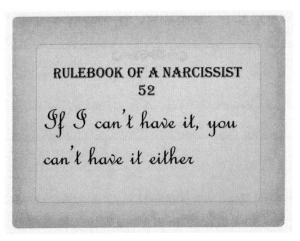

RULEBOOK OF A NARCISSIST
52

If I can't have it, you can't have it either

Narcissists are jealous.

When other people have what they want, it makes them envious as it affects their image as 'the best'. Even stronger, they will feel inferior. They feel the need to spoil experiences, ruin possessions and break up friendships to stop other people from feeling good.

Narcissists only care about themselves and have no qualms about ruining a beautiful garment in the wash, stealing someone's prized possession, stirring in a happy relationship, or creating drama to get attention. Their value of self-centredness and lack of empathy makes it easy for them to act selfishy and not feel any guilt.

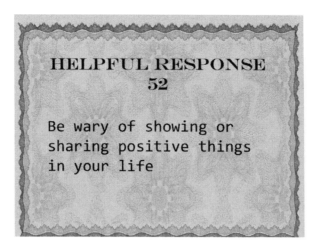

**HELPFUL RESPONSE
52**

Be wary of showing or
sharing positive things
in your life

The moment you are happy, your narcissist will be on a mission to spoil it for you.

Therefore, be selective about what you share.

Protect the positive elements in your life by keeping them to yourself or playing them down.

This relates to all elements like family, friendships, career, possessions, clothes or outings.

Be aware.

Don't be an open book. Sadly, you are pushed into behaving carefully and with suspicion, like your narcissist. This is a challenge as dealing with a narcissist often means you have to violate your own values.

RULEBOOK OF A NARCISSIST
53

We have the best relationship in the world. Everybody envies us

Narcissists embrace the idea that their relationship is the best one possible. They are charming, endearing, returning back to the love bombing state, to convince their partner how well suited for each other they are.

Photographs show them as lovingly holding their partner's hand, staring into their eyes and showing off the beauty of the relationship.

They love to share on social media their holiday shots, dinner parties and anything that fits the picture perfect.

It is another mask.

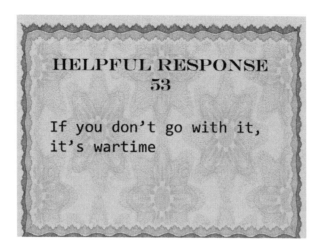

**HELPFUL RESPONSE
53**

If you don't go with it,
it's wartime

Your narcissist plays you here.

Claiming you and the relationship and playing the game of the good times.

Love bombing will always be followed by the disappointing next stage of diminishing and devaluing.

Don't get your hopes up for change.

Your narcissist will revert back to being nasty and controlling.

RULEBOOK OF A NARCISSIST
54

I mirror and copy your behaviour, text messages and ideas

Narcissists lack creativity as that means loosening a sense of control, but they can see that in certain situations their victim gets it right. When they notice that, they copy and then claim it as theirs. This could be about manners, speaking, text messages or ideas. It is the opposite of projection.

Of course, they are entitled to the glory of achievements as is part of the 'deal' in the relationship (Rule 22 'I take credits for the achievements of others').

Narcissists confuse loving with possessing and what is yours is theirs. This doesn't work both ways, as what is theirs is theirs only. They own their partners, children and everything they are, have and know.

**HELPFUL RESPONSE
54**

Your narcissist will
never accept they copied
you

Your narcissist will respond in the usual manner: lying and believing their own lies. There is nothing you can do about it.

But it can be mind-blowing and frustrating when it happens.

Don't spend any energy on it.

Best thing is to let it go.

RULEBOOK OF A NARCISSIST
55

I might leave you or I might give you another chance?

Narcissists love power games and in romantic relationships they campaign continuously to undermine the confidence of their partner.

Through techniques such as gaslighting, put downs, lying and reframing they succeed in turning whatever confident person they started off with, into an emotionally insecure wreck.

Someone who has lost their high opinion of themselves, their sense of self and is totally co-dependent on their narcissist.

This is the position narcissists are aiming for: a partner who doesn't believe in their own value and certainly doesn't believe they will be able to survive without them.

The option of another chance will guarantee that the victim will put in even more energy to make it work. It is another game, similar to Rule 63 'You are my toy, I play with you like a cat plays with a mouse'.

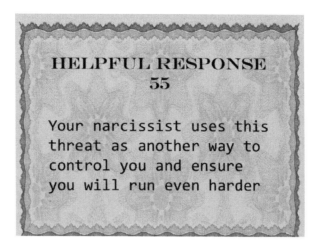

HELPFUL RESPONSE
55

Your narcissist uses this
threat as another way to
control you and ensure
you will run even harder

The fear of being left can be unbearable.

Your narcissist has campaigned to make you lose your sense of self and your confidence and become totally dependent on them.

You are in a co-dependent relationship and might feel totally devastated by the idea of the relationship ending.

You are so used to living your life through your narcissist, you can't imagine it any different.

If you recognise yourself in this situation, it will help to gently start building up your confidence and valuing yourself more.

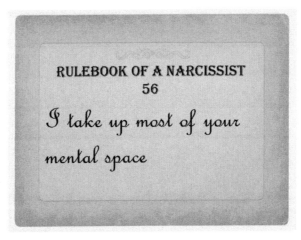

RULEBOOK OF A NARCISSIST
56

I take up most of your mental space

Narcissists infiltrate the mind of their victims through being inconsistent, unpredictable and constantly critical.

Victims feel insecure in their presence and try to make sense of what is happening through overthinking and rumination.

To stay present in their victim's mind, narcissists often send reminders through frequent text messages, random emails or phone calls.

Their unpredictable actions ensure that their victims keep ruminating, trying to make sense of it all.

It is their way to infiltrate their victim's mind and suck up their mental energy.

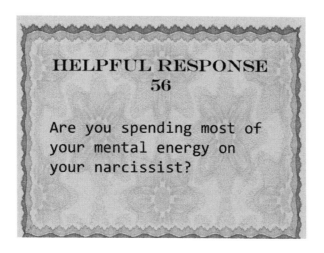

**HELPFUL RESPONSE
56**

Are you spending most of
your mental energy on
your narcissist?

Your narcissist is unpredictable, illogical, and impossible to understand. But it takes time to discover that.

Initially, you will try to comprehend their motives, reasons, and executions.

It is intriguing, challenging and captivating.

Then it becomes obsessive, frustrating, and desperate.

It is one of the ways your narcissist takes over your life.

As your narcissist has a different value system and thinking pattern, you will never be able to understand them.

You will only be able to see and predict their choices of behaviour within the context of their values.

If you know you spend too many thoughts on your narcissist, get the stop sign out and distract yourself with thoughts about something completely different.

A narcissist enters your system via the heart.
They evoke warmth and even love,
and you open up to them. Like an octopus they
wriggle their way up from your heart into your
head, where they absorb your thoughts and
replace them with their toxic ideas. By then they
have captured your head and heart and keep you
in position with their multiple tentacles.

You are lost.

> **RULEBOOK OF A NARCISSIST**
> **57**
>
> *Our relationship is conditional. If you obey me, I will accept you*

Life is one big negotiation.

Narcissists will never give anything for free.

If people want something from them, they have to deserve it.

Or it becomes an exchange.

It is always 'quid pro quo' – something for something, like a business arrangement.

The big condition they put on their victims is their demand to be obeyed, which is another way of controlling.

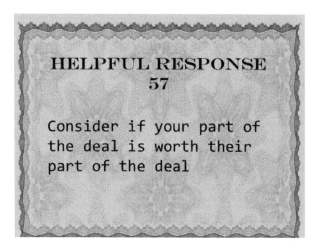

HELPFUL RESPONSE
57

Consider if your part of the deal is worth their part of the deal

Often your narcissist will have manipulated you in a situation of giving without you even realising it.

Take a step back and notice what you are giving in the relationship.

And then notice what you are getting back.

Is there equality?

Is it in balance?

If not, consider what would create more balance for you and how you could achieve that.

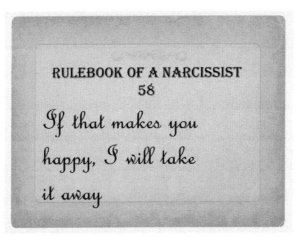

RULEBOOK OF A NARCISSIST
58

If that makes you happy, I will take it away

Narcissists are not only always the best, they also want the best for themselves.

They don't really know happiness or unhappiness. They just know the satisfaction of outshining others and therefore feeling superior.

When someone is happy, narcissists don't really understand that, but are annoyed as it seems that others are in a better place.

How could that be possible?

For narcissists it is unthinkable and unacceptable.

There is only one answer and that is to destroy whatever is bringing happiness.

It is easy for them as 'I am the only one that is important' and there is no empathy.

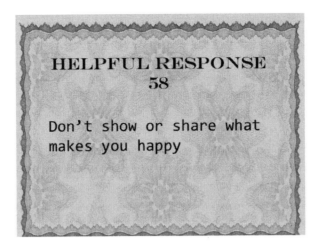

**HELPFUL RESPONSE
58**

Don't show or share what
makes you happy

Your narcissist is cruel and has no qualms about destroying what makes you happy.

They will kill your pet, break your possessions or destroy your friendships.

Whatever has value to you is a threat to the importance of your narcissist.

You are spending your energy on something other than them and that is unacceptable.

The fewer things you have to get positive energy from, the better victim material you are.

To keep yourself protected, don't show or share what makes you happy.

My mother told me my house wasn't ready for the baby.

I knew, but I had planned to do it all during the weekend.

Putting all my love in preparing the nursery for my first born. I was so excited.

When I was at work, my mother sneaked in and did it all for me.

She presented it as a nice surprise.

But she robbed me from my experience of doing it myself.

I hated her for doing that.

I know she loved that I hated her.

RULEBOOK OF A NARCISSIST
59

Your behaviour sparks my behaviour. If you don't like mine, change yours

This is the logic of narcissists and their inability to take responsibility.

Not even for their own behaviour.

If they are criticised about their behaviour, they immediately make someone else accountable.

They are always right and therefore don't see the need to consider their impact on the situation.

When a man hit his partner and she said what he did was wrong, he answered: 'You behaved appalling and made me smack you. You did it to yourself'.

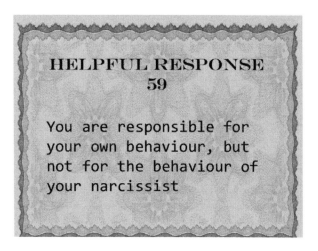

HELPFUL RESPONSE
59

You are responsible for
your own behaviour, but
not for the behaviour of
your narcissist

Your narcissist manipulates the situation and hands over the responsibility and the guilt to you.

Your narcissist wants you to take the blame.

'I am late because you didn't wake me up'

Are you their alarm clock?

'I am fat because you are a crap cook'

Are you responsible for each bite they take?

'I feel ill because you don't look after me.'

Are you responsible for their lifestyle choices?

Ask yourself 'Is this my responsibility?' and if it isn't, there is no reason to feel guilty.

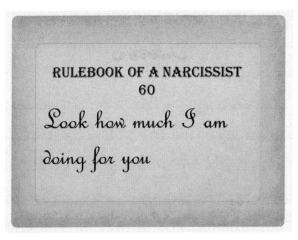

**RULEBOOK OF A NARCISSIST
60**

Look how much I am doing for you

Narcissists love to sing their own praises and are always exaggerating what they do for others.

They don't do it because they want to be kind.

They only do it to make a positive impression on others.

Narcissists will do charity work if it shows them in a good light.

They want others to think about them as special and great.

When they say 'look what I am doing for you' they are saying, reward me for what I am doing: give me attention, be grateful, tell me how great I am, because that is the only reason I am doing things for you.

It is like a business deal, where 'I don't care about you, I only care about me'.

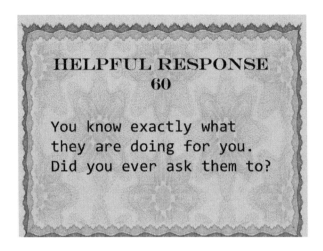

HELPFUL RESPONSE
60

You know exactly what
they are doing for you.
Did you ever ask them to?

Your narcissist wants you to be grateful at least, but even better to feel guilty and that you owe them.

Creating an imbalance that makes them superior.

Expecting you to put more effort into accommodating them.

Running their errands, singing their praises and living for them.

Did you ever ask them to do things for you?

Did they really do what they say they did?

Often your narcissist blows their actions out of proportion or they just lie and say that they did something for you.

They will only take action for their own benefit.

Ask yourself if you really owe your narcissist.

Whenever his girlfriend was adamant to lose weight,

He bought her favourite chocolate

When his girlfriend had a big presentation the next day,

He cooked her a surprise romantic dinner

When his girlfriend planned a night out with her friends,

He fell terribly ill and couldn't be by himself

When his girlfriend bought a great garment,

He washed it too hot and ruined it

When his girlfriend got angry with him because

she didn't feel supported,

He called her negative and critical

RULEBOOK OF A NARCISSIST
61
I move the goalposts
whenever it suits me

Narcissists easily change their ideas and requirements.

It is to suit them and their situation, but also to create confusion.

What they wanted yesterday is not important today.

Today it is something different.

They are unreliable and can change within a second.

Forcing others to walk on eggshells.

Always to serve their own purpose.

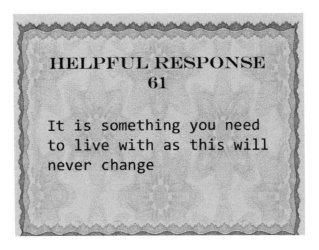

**HELPFUL RESPONSE
61**

It is something you need
to live with as this will
never change

Your narcissist wants to keep you on your toes, focusing on them and thinking about them and their wishes all the time.

What better way to do that than to confuse you?

It is also a means to test you.

Did you listen?

Did you pick up on their ideas and wishes?

You can never really relax as you never know where the goalposts are.

You have to accept that you will never 'know'.

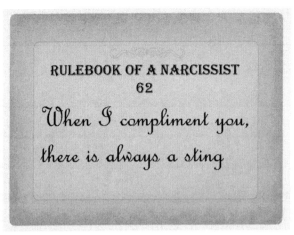

RULEBOOK OF A NARCISSIST
62

When I compliment you, there is always a sting

Narcissists can't do compliments as that would be admitting that someone else is better than they are.

If they make a kind remark it will be balanced by an unkind one.

Narcissists are brilliant at this: 'Your hair has a great shape, shame it's the wrong colour'.

They don't want to make others feel good, they only want to upset or confuse them.

The push and pull, positive followed by negative, lifting up and breaking down, they do that very well.

HELPFUL RESPONSE
62

You can't trust a
compliment or positive
comment

There will be a nasty side to it, even if you are not aware of it in the first instance.

If that is the case, wait for the put down, as it is on its way.

When you can't find the sting, it might be in the compliment itself.

If your narcissist thinks your dress makes you look ugly, they might tell you how lovely it is. You wearing that dress serves the purpose that you won't outshine them.

The compliment might also be an investment into a repayment later.

'You look lovely' as the foreplay for intimacy.

Always be prepared for the put down, so you won't be taken by surprise.

> **RULEBOOK OF A NARCISSIST**
> **63**
>
> *You are my toy, I play with you like a cat plays with a mouse*

Narcissists love to play power games.

Like a cat who has caught a mouse, then hits it lightly so it squeaks and then waits till it is silent, to touch it again, relishing in the reaction.

They enjoy this immensely.

It's cruel and they can do it because they lack empathy and don't really care that they cause pain to others.

It is an also an example of Schadenfreude (Rule 5 'I thrive on the misery of others').

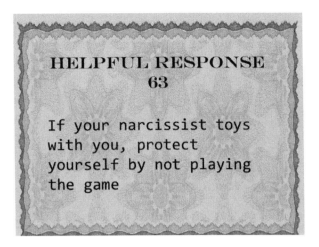

**HELPFUL RESPONSE
63**

If your narcissist toys
with you, protect
yourself by not playing
the game

Your narcissist wants you to squeak and react.

This will give them the thrill they are looking for.

If you become disengaged and don't react, there is nothing to be gained for them.

They will soon look for another victim or another way to feel powerful.

I am not crying because of you;
You are not worth it.
I am crying because of me;
At last, I recognize my value.

7

ABC of narcissism

What follows here is a glossary of commonly used terms regarding narcissism.

Admiration

Narcissists love to be admired. 'You are so special, good, intelligent... '.

It makes them happy and gets everyone off the hook.

For a while.

Attention

Attention is balsam for the soul of narcissists. They need it. They will look for it and even manufacture it. That is why they make scenes at weddings, funerals and parties where other people would normally be getting all the attention.

Blaming

Narcissists don't take responsibility for their choices and actions.

Just as Pinocchio has a big nose to point out he is lying; narcissists have a huge index finger to point at someone else to blame.

Boundaries

Victims of narcissists can fight back, trying to take some control by setting boundaries. In the eyes of narcissists, boundaries are there to be challenged and preferably broken.

Bread crumbing

Narcissists send out flirtatious but non-committal social signals. They confuse, only go for last minute dates, send inconsistent messages, and won't let their 'partner' go completely, always keeping a little carrot dangling.

Bullying

Bullying is a pattern of repeatedly and deliberately harming and humiliating others, specifically those who are vulnerable. A common trait of narcissists.

Co-dependency

Co-dependency is about absorbing someone else, merging two individuals into one. A co-dependent person can't function on their own and their thoughts and behaviours are always informed by someone else. The victims of narcissists become so intoxicated that they live for and through them. Narcissists are so scared to lose their supply source that they often become co-dependent as well.

Cognitive dissonance

When events are not in line with your values, ideas or opinions, it is upsetting and causes stress, anxiety and low self-worth. Rather than addressing the root cause, which is advisable, people then create a narrative which reduces the upset and makes the event more acceptable.

Coercive control

Coercive control is a strategic pattern of behaviour designed to exploit, control, create dependency and dominate. The victim's everyday existence is micro-managed, limited and controlled by narcissists.

Covert narcissism

When narcissists are not 'in your face' but showing passive aggression, victim behaviour, doing 'good' to enhance their image and using more subtle methods to have their needs met. It is more difficult to recognise them as a narcissist.

My boyfriend always confused me.

Let's talk openly. I want to know your feelings.

Then I opened up and told him what I felt.

He then said he totally got it, as he felt the same.

And continued talking on about himself.

Any conversation always was about him.

Delusional

Delusional is the state of mind where someone can't tell what's real and what is imagined. Narcissists twist the truth to suit their agenda and they are convinced about the truth of what they portray.

Divide and conquer

The manipulation technique applied by Julius Caesar and Napoleon in wartime: create confusion and turn your enemies against each other, then come in to beat them up and create order and rule over your weakened opponents. Narcissists are good at that in family and close friendship situations.

Emotional disengagement

Emotional disengagement is the ability to block emotions in order to protect yourself from unwanted abuse, drama, anxiety or stress (see grey rocking).

Emotionally unavailable

People who can't access their emotions can't be part of an emotional relationship or emotional intimacy. This apply to narcissists.

Emotions: anger, fear, hate, jealousy

These emotions carry low vibrational energies, which means they are heavy and might feel like a burden. They push people down. These are the only emotions known to narcissists. These emotions fulfil the purpose of protecting the fragile ego and forcing others to offer Narcissistic Supply.

Empaths

Empaths are highly empathic people, more tuned into the needs of others, than their own. Narcissists are attracted to empaths, who are excellent targets for control, as they are open to forgiving, taking the blame, choosing peace and making others more important than themselves.

Entitlement

Believing you have a right to something … without the need to actually deserve it. Narcissists are entitled to whatever they want: attention, services, sex, money and more.

Fluffing up

The technique to 'mellow' narcissists for your benefits. 'Manipulating the manipulator'. Pay them compliments, be caring, make a fuss, with the purpose of making them do what you want.

Flying monkeys

Narcissists recruit people who seem happy to accommodate them to do their dirty work and form an information network. Flying monkeys are flattered to be chosen, never critical and act on behalf of a narcissist.

Fragile ego

Underneath the arrogance, bragging and cockiness is a feeling of being inadequate, unlovable, and incompetent. Normal people will seek to address these issues in therapy or coaching, but narcissists have chosen to hide this fragility and work their whole life to avoid being exposed.

Future faking

Narcissists make promises about possibilities in the future to get what they want in the present. 'Next time' and 'It will be so much better once this is over'.

Gaslighting

A form of psychological abuse. Narcissists are very skilful at it. It is done by continuously challenging someone's remarks, observations and thoughts in order to make them doubt their reality. It makes their victims feel confused, anxious, and lose trust in themselves.

Grandiosity

Typical for narcissists: an exaggerated sense of one's own importance, power, knowledge, or identity, even if there is little evidence to support these beliefs.

Grey rocking

Taking the attitude of not taking any interest and becoming unresponsive. An attempt to keep yourself emotionally safe from the actions and words of narcissists. But equally to encourage them to lose interest because of a lack of Narcissistic Supply.

Hypervigilance

A state of increased alertness, where someone is extremely sensitive to their surroundings, and super alert to hidden dangers. Like constantly walking on very breakable eggshells. After time, this happens to most victims of abuse.

Infidelity

The lack of love and loyalty makes it easy for narcissists to get more supply via a range of sexual relationships, regardless of whether they are in a marriage or partnership.

Jealousy

Narcissists can't handle it when other people seem to be better than they are. This sparks their jealousy.

Lying

Narcissists can't be trusted. The best attitude to everything they say is to check it out for yourself.

Malignant narcissist

Narcissism is a spectrum and malignant narcissists are the most dangerous as they thrive on causing suffering in others. Their lack of empathy and emotional awareness means they lack a conscience or feelings of guilt. This makes them extremely cruel.

Manipulation

Techniques to control the thoughts and actions of others. Narcissists have a huge toolkit of manipulation techniques.

Mask

Narcissists confuse others as they portray themselves differently in private and in public. Their mask is charming, generous and fun. Their real self is nasty, mean and manipulative. Most people only know them through their mask and won't understand the stories of victims.

Narcissistic rage

An extremely intense anger and rage which is fuelled by the fear of discovery. It is terrifying to be on the receiving end. It can involve physical violence and abuse.

No contact

When victims remove themselves from the influence of narcissists, the advisable route to go is 'no contact', cutting all the cords. Narcissists will try to manipulate their victims back into their lives, as the 'no contact' decision is perceived as a defeat and rejection.

Overt narcissism

Narcissists who present themselves with arrogance and an inflated sense of self. They are easy to recognise and don't care if they are called a 'narcissist'.

Passive aggression

Passive-aggressive behaviour is a pattern of indirectly expressing negative feelings instead of openly addressing them. Being suggestive, dismissive facial expressions and diminishing remarks in order to put someone down without being openly nasty and accountable. Narcissists are experts in applying passive aggression.

Post-traumatic stress disorder (PTSD)

Can happen to a person after experiencing a traumatic event or continuous exposure to a series of smaller traumas which has caused them to feel fearful, shocked or helpless. Long-term effects include hypervigilance, flashbacks, difficulty sleeping and anxiety.

Projection

This is a defence mechanism used to cope with difficult feelings or emotions. Psychological projection involves projecting these feelings or emotions onto someone else, rather than admitting to or dealing with them. Narcissists will often accuse their victims of what they are doing wrong themselves.

Quarrel

To be avoided at all costs with narcissists. They can't handle criticism and will see a disagreement as a dismissal of them 'being the best'. It might lead to narcissistic rage, punishment and stronger control.

Reframing

Reframing is a technique used to help create a different way of looking at a situation, person or relationship by changing its meaning. Narcissists will do this to change the perspective. Especially if the original 'frame' makes someone else looks good, they are keen to reframe it to make them look bad.

Scapegoating

In families with narcissistic parents, often one of the children will be singled out to be mistreated. The other family members may well go along with this as it is their way to survive. The other roles for the children are the golden child and the invisible one.

Smear campaign

Smear campaigns aim to damage someone's reputation. Narcissists will smear others for a variety of reasons: alienation from family and friends, punishment and control.

Stonewalling or silent treatment

Stonewalling is the refusal to communicate with someone, giving them the silent treatment. It is one of the most prevalent narcissistic abuse techniques and can last for weeks.

Trauma bond

Trauma bonding is a psychological survival response to abuse. It occurs when the victim develops or holds onto unhealthy and inappropriate feelings for their abuser: feeling sorry for them, wanting to rescue them, and developing an attachment. It often goes together with co-dependency. The trauma bond becomes a physical addiction when fear is counteracted by the delight and relief after the abusive explosion through happy hormones dopamine and oxytocin.

Triangulation

Triangulation is a manipulation tactic where narcissists will talk on behalf of others. 'He said this about you'. Narcissists use this tactic to confuse people and alienate them from each other so they can take control.

Unpredictability

This is a power tool of narcissists and puts their victims on high alert.
All the time.

Victim behaviour

Narcissists will portray themselves as victims, in order to get other people to do things for them, receive the sympathy vote and not take responsibility. They will blame others.

Word salad

Narcissists create word salads as a form of gaslighting, using language. It is about throwing words around, undermining what someone is saying, ignoring reasons and facts, but keeping on talking in their own line of thoughts to numb their listener.

Xenophobia

Xenophobia is a fear of people from other countries, but is usually applied in the context of racism. Research shows that most racists share strong narcissistic tendencies.

You

For narcissists it is all about I, myself, and me. And never ever about you. They don't really see a person, they see functionality, as in: 'How can you serve me? And then, do you really serve me?' The moment you don't serve their purpose, they are off to replace you with the next person.

Zipping up

One way of protecting yourself against the influences of a narcissist is by using the technique of zipping up as described in Chapter 8 on tools and techniques.

Before you offer more to your narcissist, ask yourself 5 questions:

o What does it give me?
o What does it take from me?
o Who benefits?
o Who pays the price?
o Is it my responsibility?

8

Tools and techniques to deal with narcissists

Introduction

This book aims to inform about day to day situations. However, I couldn't resist offering a few suggestions of tools and techniques which are effective when dealing with narcissists and other challenging people. I offer a wider range of tools in my book *From Victim to Victor – Narcissism Survival Guide*.

1 Protect – zipping up

This simple technique from Donna Eden (energy practitioner) can help you protect yourself. It is as if you create an energy shield between yourself and others. The subtle energy of your hand creates protection to your central nervous system. Take a deep breath as you do this and trust that you are protected.

+ Stand straight and tap firmly the soft spot under your collar bones on both sides.

+ While you breathe out spread arms and scoop the air around you.

+ Bring hands to pubic bone.

+ While breathing in bring hands to your mouth.

+ Repeat three times.

Apply this technique as often as required.

2 Communicate – JADE

When people are insecure, they usually present their choices and decisions with a lot of background information: a detailed explanation, some extra information, pros and cons, the thinking process, and more irrelevant details.

In a relationship with a narcissist, you will be the one who is insecure and possibly fearful when talking about one of your decisions.

Providing a detailed justification will help you to feel more secure, but you are only giving them the ammunition they need to challenge you.

You don't owe anyone a reason for your choices. No one has the right to challenge you if you don't want to be challenged.

The way to prevent the challenge is JADE, which is one of the best tools to communicate clearly without fear or doubt.

JADE stands for DO NOT:

Justify

Argue

Defend

Explain

The narcissist is always looking to undermine you and will use the information in your justification, defence, or explanation to start challenging your decision. You make it easy for them to start an argument, using your own words.

To avoid these situations, apply JADE whenever you can.

3 Process – subconscious writing

Downloading your thoughts is a tool to gain clarity without focused thinking. The suggestion is to do this daily for 20 minutes. Just pick up a pen and start writing without lifting your pen off the paper. The unconscious stream that flows forth is of great value in processing what is happening in our life. Don't stop writing, no matter what emerges from the tip of your pen, until you finish your 20 minutes. If some thoughts try to intrude, just go with those, and write them down.

Remember: no one ever needs to read these pages, including you.

Thought downloading pages is a particularly good tool if you have conscious (or subconscious) worries, psychic wounds, fears, or other concerns that you may be ignoring or suppressing. Bringing them to the surface and getting them down on paper helps reduce anxiety and stops energy from being lost to unproductive thoughts and feelings (a word of caution: this can be emotionally draining).

Writing down your thoughts as they appear can help to lift their burden from your mind. This is a way of decluttering. You are tidying up your mental desk so that you can do more important work.

Let your thoughts speak for themselves.

Coaching for narcissistic abuse recovery

When it comes to healing from narcissistic abuse we are talking about a journey of transformation. Learning how to change the focus of attention from the external to the internal.

For years, the external focus was your narcissist and their wishes, and it seems to have become ingrained to keep that external focus. Not being validated and valued by others, including yourself, seems to make it very difficult to tuning into your authentic self. And become your own focus of attention.

Then of course, there is the trauma and the post-traumatic stress disorder which you are still carrying. The pain, the guilt and the anxiety for 'doing it wrong', the hunger for love and the sadness of failure are all residues of the abuse.

When facing your transformation, it is important to work with someone who fully understands the type of abuse and the challenges that come with it. I used my personal and professional experience to design the journey for narcissistic abuse recovery coaching and defined a programme of five steps:

1. Understanding narcissistic personality disorder and the traits, values and thinking patterns of your narcissist(s).

2. Becoming aware of how your narcissist(s) has impacted your life, thoughts, emotions and behaviour. Then and now: trauma, post-traumatic stress disorder, cognitive dissonance, confidence, self-neglect and more.

3. Learning skills to deal with narcissistic abusive traits.

4. Building up self-knowledge and awareness.

5. Developing a loving and respectful relationship with yourself.

Recovery is an organic process, and you will jump between different steps. While you are learning more about your narcissist, you might also become aware of their influence on your emotions and build up self-knowledge at the same time.

Cathy Beetz had only four sessions and this is what she had to say:

'When I happened upon Mariette's book while browsing Amazon, I was impressed with the reviews so decided to order because I suspected that I was dealing with a narcissist at work (my boss). In one section, there is a quiz you can take to determine if the person who is hurting you is a narcissist. When I took the quiz about my boss, it was plain as day that that's what I had on my hands. I had been in a couple romantic relationships with narcissists, so I knew the signs. A narcissistic boss is different from a narcissistic husband/ boyfriend, but they are all abusive. After reading the book, I decided to take advantage of the free first coaching session with Mariette via Zoom. I was able to 'unload' on her while she listened the entire time. I decided to continue her sessions, and after only a couple months, I was able to use a few different, but very effective methods to close my emotional self off from my boss, even while physically being with her. Mariette's coaching helped me to transform myself (because, of course, you cannot change your narcissist) enough that I had the courage to apply for another job within the same company, and I got it! I start on Monday and thank God every day that I found Mariette and her book. It has truly changed my life!!'

Conclusion

After '*From Victim to Victor – Narcissism Survival Guide*' was published in June 2020, I believed I was done. I had shared my personal experience and professional knowledge and knew it would help others.

How could I have known the rollercoaster I was embarking on?

The number of people reaching out to me, because – after reading mine – their story at last made sense. I have met hundreds of people since then and supported clients in their process of healing from narcissistic abuse.

My mission is to educate others on narcissism. Knowledge is power and the more we know, the less likely we are to become a victim.

I aim to educate in a straightforward and accessible format. Offering information that is simple to comprehend and apply.

The rulebook seemed a light way of presenting heavy duty material, and my wish is that you have a much better understanding of the way narcissists operate. I would love it when you leave a review on Amazon.

If you found this book informative, you will benefit from reading my other one too. It offers a 50 traits checklist to guide you through recognising your narcissist and the ways you have been affected by them.

What's next?

If it is part of your journey to move away from your narcissist, you are in for a challenge. And there is no need to do it all by yourself.

Find a coach or counsellor who is a specialist in this area and can support you.

Join my Facebook group: Narcissism, from victim to surviving to thriving.

Book a free coaching call with me to get advice on your next step: https://mariettejansen-coaching.youcanbook.me/

You are not alone, and you don't have to make the journey all by yourself.

All my love,

Mariette

If you enjoyed this book, please consider leaving a review on Amazon. It will make it easier to find for people who would benefit from it.

About the author

Mariette Jansen is a life coach, psychotherapist, blogger and speaker.

Mariette obtained a PhD in Communication Science in The Netherlands and for several years worked in corporate organisations. An opportunity to retrain arose after the birth of her eldest son, when she qualified as a psychotherapist, a counselling tutor and a meditation teacher. After ten years, she decided to focus her client work more on action and goals and has worked since 2011 as a successful life coach.

Mariette always knew that something wasn't right, but couldn't pinpoint what it was. Her parents kept on telling her she was the one who was wrong. But Mariette knew it couldn't be just her.

Growing up in a dysfunctional family took its toll. One of Mariette reactions to her situation was to develop an eating disorder, bulimia nervosa, which lasted 22 years.

Although Mariette now realises that she grew up in a narcissistic family, she only started to understand the full extent of her situation in her late 50s. Her mother, her main narcissist, was the most important person in her life and most of her actions were inspired by the wish to please her and be on the receiving end of love, acceptance and respect. It never happened.

As a result of her own realisation, Mariette discovered narcissism and how it plays out. It was an eye-opener and a sanity-saver.

All of a sudden, clarity hit and life made sense. It got easier to understand how to deal with it all and apply the behaviours that would support her ongoing happiness and well-being.

How to contact Dr Mariette Jansen

Email: mariette@drdestress.co.uk

Website: www.drdestress.co.uk

LinkedIn: www.linkedin.com/in/mariettejansendrdestress/

Bibliography

Books

Arabi, Shahida (2017). *Power: Surviving and thriving after narcissistic abuse.* New York: Thought Catalog Books.

Bradshaw, John (1933). *The family: A new way of creating solid self-esteem.* Deerfield Beach Florida: Health Communications Inc.

Carnes, Patrick J (2017). *The Betrayal Bond.* Deerfield Beach Florida: Health Communications Inc.

Gosbee, Karen (2020). *A Perfect Nightmare.* Toronto: Sutherland House.

Hatfield, E., Cacioppo, J. T. and Rapson, R. L. (1994). *Emotional contagion.* Cambridge: Cambridge University Press.

Jansen, Mariette (2020). *From Victim to Victor – Narcissism Survival Guide.* London: Indie Publishing.

Jackson, Theresa (2017). *How to handle a narcissist.* Indie Publishers.

Jeffers, Susan (1991). *Feel the fear and do it anyway.* London: Arrow Books.

Marsh, Abigail (2017). *The fear factor: How one emotion connects altruists, psychopaths, and everyone in-between.* New York: Basic Books.

Stewart, Ian & Joines, Vann (1987). *TA today: A new introduction to transactional analysis.* Nottingham: Lifespace Publishing.

Weblinks

www.drsyrasderksen.com/blog/seeing-narcissism-in-the-brain

https://psychcentral.com/blog/new-research-may-support-the-existence-of-empaths/

www.lifeadvancer.com/empaths-and-narcissists-attraction/

Printed in Great Britain
by Amazon